The Second Start

Finding Joy in the New You

Tammy Lee Schumacher

Published by Best Seller Publishing®, Pasadena, CA
Best Seller Publishing® is a registered trademark
Printed in the United States of America.
ISBN 978-1-946978-22-6

This publication is designed to provide accurate and authoritative information with regard to the subject matter covered. It is sold with the understanding that the publisher is not engaged in rendering legal, accounting, or other professional advice. If legal advice or other expert assistance is required, the services of a competent professional should be sought. The opinions expressed by the authors in this book are not endorsed by Best Seller Publishing® and are the sole responsibility of the author rendering the opinion.

Most Best Seller Publishing® titles are available at special quantity discounts for bulk purchases for sales promotions, premiums, fundraising, and educational use. Special versions or book excerpts can also be created to fit specific needs.

For more information, please write:
Best Seller Publishing®
1346 Walnut Street, #205
Pasadena, CA 91106
or call 1(626) 765 9750
Toll Free: 1(844) 850-3500
Visit us online at: www.BestSellerPublishing.org

Credit for Front and Back cover photos goes to the Outstanding Ashlee Dephillippo

Praise for "The Second Start"

The Second Start is an explosive, honest and orgasmic roller coaster of a read with the fun and loving Tammy Lee. It's insightful, packed with women's wisdom and a book who's time has come right in just the the knick of time. Tammy's refreshing outlook and honesty makes her work easy and fun to digest and packs a punch that you will surely remember. This book is for you if you're READY to take a stand for your purpose, find your inner compass, voice and power and let her rip! No more appologies, no more playing small. With Tammy's guidance and clever tips on how to HAVE IT ALL, the romance, the career and the woman you've always wanted to be - you'll get into ACTION and follow her step by step plan for creating the life you've always imagined.

VANESSA SIMPKINS
Best Selling Author of "Take Your Power Back Now: The Ultimate Confidence Guide for Women", Founder of the SoulSister Mastermind Experience & The 10k in 30 Day Program

www.TakeYourPowerBackNow.com

Quite often people allow their negative past to hold them from reaching happiness & harmony with one's self. I have known Tammy Lee for over 20 years now. I have watched her transformation from being a timid uncertain woman to a person of strength and conviction. Her courage to tap into her inner self, embracing her past and overcoming those things that held her back is amazing. I would encourage anyone to allow Tammy Lee to hold their hand and let her incredible spirit guide them past the obstacles that keep you from the joy we so richly deserve.

SCOTT BEHAN
Author and Entrepreneur

"You are a Wedge Buster Tammy, the world needs you, we need you. Tammy we need all of you, even your weird self. Tammy the world needs you!"
Bo Eason
www.boeason.com

Ever since I have known Tammy Lee she has been completely committed to self-realization and growth, and carrying the message of empowerment of self, esp. of women into the world. This book is the fruits of Tammy's commitment to sharing her own story to help and encourage others with this core message: if I can you can. I highly recommend this very personal and "real life hands you challenges" story no matter if you want to just delve into someone else's courageous life or take away something you can apply in your own situation.

Claudia Mardel
Author, Healer, Teacher and Pottery from the Soul Creator
www.claudiamardel.com and www.radiantsoul.org

Read this book like it is the one that can transform you and your relationship from sadness, disappointment, despair, and hopelessness to JOY and HAPPINESS. Tammy and Tim, with God's help and guidance, faced and confronted the darkest days of their marriage in order to help others who have lost hope and who fear the destruction of their marriage and family with the burden of children accepting a broken family. Their journey through the darkness brings light to all those who are committed to winning in their relationship. This book is about winning!

Drs. Melvin and Sherrie Allen
Relationship Experts
Certified Myers Briggs Practitioners
Prepare-Enrich facilitators

"Tammy, you have come through some dark spots and triumphed. Your laugh testifies to the joys you know now. This book shares your trials and leads by example."

ROBERT G. ALLEN
#1 New York Times bestselling author

En Joy the Journey

Tammy Lee Schunker

You Are Loved

This book is dedicated to My Family:

My husband Tim

and

Our five children

Joey

Crystal

Shanna

Jenna

Tara

The Legacy of Real Love forever lives!!!

Table of Content

CHAPTER 1   Beginning Times 1

CHAPTER 2   My High School Years.............................11

CHAPTER 3   My Wedding Night 19

CHAPTER 4   New Life...27

CHAPTER 5   Joey 35

CHAPTER 6   Pregnant Teen..43

CHAPTER 7   Look After Yourself First 49

CHAPTER 8   Foundation Building 57

CHAPTER 9   The Birthday..65

CHAPTER 10   The Elephant in the Room....................71

CHAPTER 11   Slipping Away 77

CHAPTER 12   Turning the Corner................................85

CHAPTER 13   No Elephants..95

CHAPTER 14   Leaving 105

CHAPTER 15   The Papers Arrive...................................111

CHAPTER 16   Melvin and Sherrie................................121

CHAPTER 17   64 Chevy 129

CHAPTER 18 New Floor 135

CHAPTER 19 Take Care of Yourself 143

CHAPTER 20 Ask Me 151

CHAPTER 21 The Rough Spot 157

CHAPTER 22 Get Back On...163

CHAPTER 23 Real Communication 171

CHAPTER 24 The Greatest Present 177

CHAPTER 25 Creating Heaven on Earth.......................185

WORK WITH TAMMY: Women, Your Time Is Now –
Your Sisters Are waiting for You to arrive! 189

CHAPTER 1
Beginning Times

I started off my years in the small town in Otis, Kansas, just a couple of blocks away from my grandmother's two-storey red brick home with a big open porch out front. I can still remember skipping along hand-in-hand with my older sister Cindy, down the sidewalk in our pretty dresses. I still remember feeling like a princess — so pretty in my frilly blue dress, as it bounced up and down. We giggled together and I was so happy. I must have been about two at the time, according to my mother, who found it hard believe that I could remember times when I was so young. We were either going to church or over to Grandma's. We moved away when I was three, to Hays, Kansas, where I finished growing up and going to school.

Cindy was so smart in school. She never had to study and always got straight A's. She was also the best at sports and playing games. It seemed as if she could never lose at anything. I really looked up to her when I was in grade school. Karen, my little sister, was always quiet and kept to herself. It feels odd and a bit sad to me that I cannot remember doing much with her, as if we both missed out on something special.

We grew up in the best neighborhood ever, playing at the playground down the block, staying up late during summer evenings with all the neighbor kids playing Hide N Go Seek, Red Rover, Green Light-Red Light, going swimming, walking to the movies two miles away, going to the drive-in theater, having a blast at the sidewalk bazaar in downtown Main Street. My mom worked in the summers and gave us an allowance so we had money for movie tickets and to get treats at the local five and dime store. Summers were pretty wonderful. Even with all of that, maybe because I was the middle child, I always felt alone, a bit lost, like I never belonged. Cindy was Daddy's girl and Karen was Mom's baby girl. I would wonder at times if I was adopted, and I would pray for my real parents to come and whisk me away.

Every Sunday we would load up in the car and drive the 30 minutes to Grandma's. Yum yum, Grandma's chicken and noodles were our main Sunday dinner. Made from scratch, it was the family favorite, licking the plate clean good, yep. My sisters and I were Grandma's pride and joy. She loved us unconditionally. Grandma's gardens were always bursting with strawberries and beautiful gladiolas. Wow, those flowers were taller than me, and I was amazed by them. Every time I see glads, I instantly remember my grandma, my love.

Over the years, the families grew. My dad was the oldest of six boys, and Sundays at Grandma's remained the place for us all to come together, the men always watching their Sunday football. The little girl in me found them boring, so we made our own fun.

All three of us girls always wanted so much for our dad to be proud of us, to win his approval. When we were old enough to participate in sports, Dad took us to get our ball gloves and made sure they were fitted just right to our hands, and helped us to pick out the right bat so we could hit those home runs. Not long after that it was time for our bicycles. Again it was Dad who took us to get them at the local Tempo store. I was proud as ever riding my yellow ten-speed, attempting to race Cindy on her red one. She won of course. Her long legs were her advantage.

As a grade school child, I could never understand why Mom always seemed to be walking on egg shells around Dad. She was always trying to make sure he was pleased. She always put his needs before ours. I remember thinking to myself, if I could only make Mom and Dad laugh, everything would be okay, like *I Love Lucy* made us laugh when we watched on Monday nights when Dad was out of town working. If he was home he always watched football at that time. Secretly I always wished he was away on Monday nights, then Mom and we girls would laugh together at *I Love Lucy*.

As the peacemaker and people pleaser, always trying to make others laugh did not always work so well. The quarrelling became louder and more often, especially when there was no Squirt in the house for Dad's drinks. I still remember the rough feel of Dad's jeans' pockets as I grasped one of them and pulled with all my might, with my sisters helping me, screaming at him "No daddy don't, no daddy no daddy," as he had Mom around the neck punching her in the face.

In the summer of 1975, when I was 13, Mom and Dad's divorce finalized. We girls were asked to choose what parent we wanted to live with. That really sucked. I felt that it was easy for my sisters: Cindy with Dad and Karen with Mom. Once again, I felt lost and alone, dreading to hurt anyone's feelings by choosing.

So, I went to stay with Grandma that summer. It was a weird time in my life. I walked around in a daze. One day while at Grandma's, something happened that caused me to start laughing. I remember Grandma looking at me and exclaiming with relief in her voice, "*Now*, I got my Tammy back!"

I chose to live with Mom, thinking that my little sister Karen might need me. We moved far away from Dad and Cindy. Well, to me, the four-hour drive from Hays to Atchison was long. Back in 1975, people did not just pick up and drive that far on a whim. It was a major trip.

Karen and I rode the bus to school, scared, with no friends, the two of us at the same school but in different grades. We felt lost and alone because there were so many kids and we never saw each other during the day. Not knowing where I was going felt like being on another planet. Here I was in eighth grade, with the middle school and high school right next to each other. There were kids all over the place, and the slang they talked was hard for me to understand. One guy in my class asked me for a "piece of leg" — weird right? I found out later it meant he wanted sex. Wow, really?

Just a few days after school started, a tall black senior, Clarence, took a shine to me. "Who me?" I asked myself when he looked at me and said, "Hey, come on over here." Finally, I was no longer alone. He paid attention to me, I felt important. I must be a somebody for a senior to pick me out from all the other girls. I started going to football games to watch him play. We would meet up in the halls in-between classes for quick hellos, hugs and kisses. Actually, the kisses were after school before his practice and me getting on the bus. Then came another shock. Mom told me she was sending me back to live with my dad, telling me she cannot handle me, after she found out, from a janitor at the school, that I was kissing a black guy in the hallway. Clarence was heart-broken and wrote me a goodbye letter.

Decades later, Karen told me that it was not the janitor that told Mom on me, it was her, and that she had felt horribly guilty ever since. For more than 30 years, she felt deep guilt and that it was her fault that I left. Then she was alone.

There was no welcome for me when I went back to Hays to live with Dad and Cindy. Cindy was pissed at me and hated me for awhile, because I was entering her Queendom. It had been just her and Dad, and she loved it that way, and now I was ruining that. Sally, Dad's soon-to-be wife, also did not like me much. When she seemed to like Cindy, she was not nice to me, and If she was nice to me, she was not to Cindy. I felt I was living a hell on Earth. It's no wonder at the age of 14 I was suicidal.

The rest of my school years were about survival. Getting a job was a must as I had to pay for my own lunches and enrolments , my own clothes, everything, every single thing, except for a bra that Sally thought I should have since my well-endowed bosoms needed to be perked up.

I grew up feeling I never really fit in anywhere. Watching TV, seeing all the happy families on shows like *The Waltons*, *Little House on the Prairie*, *The Brady Bunch*, and *Happy Days*, I wondered: What was so wrong with me? Why didn't anybody love me? Why was I never important to anyone? Everyone in those shows always talked things through to work out their differences. That type of family is what I fantasized about and dreamed for. What a damn joke TV plays on us. It builds us up in our formative years with fantasies and falsities!

And where did my mom go? She never called when I was living with Dad, Sally and Cindy. No letters either. It was like I had fallen off the face of the Earth as far as she was concerned. She was living her life with her new husband, and I felt even more alone, wondering why would my mother abandon me. My 14-year-old self never understood this.

Later in life, when I asked Mom about this time, she told me that she was not sure how much to be involved with me, because there was a fine line and she was not sure where it was with Dad and Sally. Yet, as I am typing this, I think, ok this is total bullshit, because after I was out of the house, married and with children, she would come to Hays and go shopping with her girlfriend and never call me. Imagine for a moment not hearing from your mother for months at a time, and one day you're shopping and you hear her voice. I was there with two of my children, her grandchildren, and felt such shock and dismay as I looked up and said, "Mom?" And she blew me off, saying she was just "coming to town with her friend to do some shopping." To use the vernacular — what the fuck?

I still have much healing to do around events in my early childhood. I call this "the child within" healing program, something I created for myself and my clients. I am sure it was never intentional on my parents' part, yet it is my truth, and I take sole responsibility for healing those parts of me that feel that pain, that abandonment. Therefore I am self reliant, and I give my power back to myself in ways that I never realized at an earlier age that I could do.

I also found out, and have Mum's permission to say, that later when Mom and I talked about me never feeling loved growing up, she was shocked. She thought she did so much right raising us girls. However, she also said she felt the same as me growing up, never loved.

I had to grow up fast. I had my first job the summer after third grade, babysitting. It seems that once I started working, I never stopped. Maturing faster than others came along with this type of living, and when it came to boys, I couldn't stand boys my age.

They were much too immature for me. At 15, I was already going to bars. All I had to do was wear a tight shirt and I got in, because I looked 18.

Stan, who saved me from my suicidal thoughts, was the first guy in my life during that time. Unlike a lot of the others, he treated me with the utmost respect and never tried to cop a feel. I felt like a princess in his presence. It was really hard for any other guy to measure up to that, but Stan was ripped from my life when my dad told him that if he ever caught him with his 14 year old daughter again, he would throw the book at him. My heart was broken and I didn't see him again for over 17 years. He went his way and I went mine, even though we committed to stay true to each other. He would wait for me until I graduated, I would stay a virgin for him.

It was a rough summer, losing the love of my life and being called a slut and a whore by my dad, and then losing my virginity by being raped by my sister's boyfriend John, which I kept quiet about until I was in my forties. But becoming friends with Jane and Brenda helped me to create a new beginning, as did starting high school because there were more opportunities for better jobs. I switched from being a carhop at the Sonic to being one at the A & W. I enjoyed hanging out with Jane on her farm and during the few times she was able to stay in town after school. I was starting to build my own life. That was one of the biggest gifts God blessed me with, the gift of great friends. Brenda was the ornery one, just like me, and together we created some fun times. We became closer and closer as time passed, to the point that Brenda was the Godmother of my second child, Crystal. Eventually, along came Wanda, Brenda's cousin, and we too formed a wonderful friendship

I was determined that no matter what, when I had children, things would be different. My children would *all* grow up to know, to feel absolutely, within their molecules, that they are loved. They would have a place to call "home" for their remaining days — something I never had as it kept being taken away from me, first by divorce and then by my dad's wives. They would always have a Safe Haven, and if the time ever came when they would fall, there would be a safety net to catch them. I prayed for this, not just for my children but for anyone who came into my presence. I wanted all to be touched by me to some degree, that I would touch their hearts and their souls would be a bit better off for knowing me.

My grandmother was my saving grace. I believe that she is where I get the intense depth of love I have inside of me. I carry forth her unyielding pure loving heart. Her embraces were the type to melt into. I knew she shone brighter when I was around, so when I can help others to shine I feel as though I am carrying Grandma's legacy forward. I know her heart cried when the day came, in the summer of 1976, when Grandpa forced her to tell me that I could no longer stay with them, because Grandpa did not like the fact that I rode around with one of the neighbor boys.

I am here to be my children's teacher, first and foremost, not their friend, that comes later in life. I saw firsthand how a parent wanting to be their child's best friend can totally screw up the child. That was one thing I never had to worry about with my mother, and today I remain grateful for that, as she was my teacher, not my friend growing up. Even for something as simple as spelling, she would say, "Go look it up in the dictionary, sound it out." Those were her famous words and I hated it when she said that. But I learned to spell. To this day I have others, especially co-workers, asking me how to spell things. The manners Mom instilled in my sisters and me have been carried on in my children, and they carry on to my grandchildren. I also made sure I taught my kids how to do their own laundry and cook, starting with simple things. I had to know that if something ever happened to me, my children would be able to take care of themselves at a young age, especially my four girls.

Somehow I knew to allow my children to have their own voice, to share their opinions and speak up and out when necessary, even with me. The one thing I did not allow was a snotty tone or a hand raised to me. I would tell them to watch their tone and then repeat themselves. I remember the day our middle child Shanna put a sign on her bedroom door: "It is my Life…Stay Out of It." Tara, our youngest of the five, soon had one displayed on her door: "I Am a BITCH — **B**abe **I**n **T**otal **C**ontrol of **H**erself." After the shock wore off, yes, I allowed them to keep them up.

I feel like we have always had open communication. When I would pick them up from school, if I was in a bad mood I would tell them so. "Mom has had a bad day. I really need you kids to be good." To this very day, we still have very open conversations and discuss — well I think we have discussed almost every subject out there. Even sex. Some of their friends were amazed and asked to be adopted into our family.

CHAPTER 2
My High School Years

Wanda and I started hanging out more and more, and one Sunday afternoon when I called her, her brother Tim answered the phone. I knew Tim a bit because Wanda had asked him to pick me up for school a few times when my car had broken down. Since we never really talked during those times, I assumed he didn't like me or that he was annoyed because I was a pain in the ass. Anyway, Wanda was not home that Sunday, and Tim and I began to talk. I soon learned that Tim had never been mad at me. He just did not know how to talk to girls, and he liked me so much that he was scared to say anything. We talked for nearly three hours. I don't remember our conversation, but I do remember how much we laughed and felt connected — so much so that I soon broke up with my boyfriend, who just happened to be Tim's cousin, so I would be available to date Tim. I found out later from Wanda that she and her mom and dad were shocked when they walked in the door because Tim was 20 years old and had never had a girlfriend, and he had been talking to me —not just a little — but for almost three hours!

Shortly after our lengthy conversation, Tim started to show up at the A&W to get lunch when I was working my carhop job. He told me later having me bring his food out to him and seeing me walk to and away from him made his heart go pitter-patter. Before long we were hanging out a lot and eventually became a couple. Our relationship just seemed to flow into that.

For some reason Wanda was really pissed off about Tim and me dating. I thought she would be happy because she and I were best friends and now I was dating her brother. Instead she was so mad that our friendship came to a screeching halt. In P.E. class, when we played warball, she blasted those balls right at me, totally taking me off guard. After getting over my shock, I blasted them right back. The only reason I could think of was that she was jealous because Tim let me drive his truck.

Yeah, that's right, Tim let me drive his 1975 GMC, four-wheel drive, two-ton truck with straight pipes, so it was *loud* — a hotrod truck! However, he had never ever let Wanda drive it. I felt so important driving Tim's truck. That is a *big deal* for a girl to drive a guy's truck! Some would consider it even more important than wearing his class ring. During the time we were dating and knowing how much I loved motorcycles, Tim even bought a 350 Honda and would sometimes let me drive that back and forth to school.

One of the coolest things was how Tim concealed a whiskey bottle in his truck so as to not get caught with an open container of alcohol. Tim was so damn smart. He put the bottle under the hood and hooked up a tube going from the bottle and to the glove compartment — the jockey box, we called it back then. With a flip of a switch, *voilà*, whiskey was coming through the tube. This was our way to have our "mixies" while driving around. That was our main thing to do. Go to the Sonic and get a large pop and onion rings, top-off our Pepsi with some whiskey, and drive around and drag Main Street all night long, sipping our drink and eating our onion rings. I literally experienced "too much of a good thing" one night. Tim had to pull over on a side street because I'd drunk too much, and the pop and the onion rings came back up. How embarrassing, puking up on a date.

As time went on we got more and more serious, and it wasn't long before we were having sex. Imagine how embarrassed I was when I found out that my younger step-brother Andy was watching us when we were downstairs in front of the TV going at it. Andy told me later, when I was pregnant and going to marry Tim. I was shocked and I am sure I turned beat red, the little shit. Yowza.

This may sound really odd, but I never, ever thought about getting pregnant. Tim was not my first, and I had never gotten pregnant up to that point. Shortly after school started in September of my senior year, I came down with such a bad case of the flu that I was sick for almost a week, throwing up all the time. Finally one day, Sally asked me to come sit down with her and proceeded to ask if I could be pregnant. I looked at her bewildered and said "No way." She looked back and said, "Well, are you and Tim having sex?" "Um, yeah," and as I said that it dawned on me for the first time that it might not be the flu I had.

I was alone and scared walking into the doctor's appointment that Sally made for me. It was confirmed, I was pregnant. As Dr. Hull was telling me, I was shocked and even asked if he'd read the tests correctly. Nodding his head yes, he said, "Tammy, you are only 17 and you have your whole life in front of you. I suggest you have an abortion." I couldn't believe what I was hearing. I was so pissed off I felt like I was growing claws out of my fingers. I wanted to rip his head off and kick him in the nuts. I walked out of his office and never saw him again. I could never trust him after that conversation. "What if he would intentionally do something to hurt my baby?" That thought was among the many that were screaming in my head. All on my own, a scared 17-year-old pregnant girl, I found a wonderful doctor soon afterwards, Dr. Mickey Myrick.

I completely agree with any of you who are thinking, "How the heck did Tammy not think she could get pregnant?" I really do not know the answer. In some ways I was naive. It just never crossed my mind with Tim. I never considered going on the pill because cancer ran in my family on my mom's side, and from an early age all I ever heard about being on the pill was about the cancer risks. I didn't have anybody to talk to about things like this. I was mostly scared of getting cancer from being on the pill.

The day I found out I was pregnant I went home to tell my dad, and even though I was petrified to do it, I was overwhelmed at how well he took it and how supportive he was and how he hugged me and told me that everything was going to be okay.

It didn't take long for people to start noticing and talking about the fact that I was pregnant. I had to tell my teachers and rearrange my schedules. Being due in May, I had to make sure that all my credits to graduate were met before then. Even though I felt odd and out of place at school, I kept my focus on graduating and I kept even more to myself. If you were pregnant in high school 30 some years ago, often your parents would send you off to have your baby somewhere else, as if they were ashamed of you. I cannot imagine that.

Mrs. Zee Neely, my senior English teacher, was remarkable with me. I would never have thought that one of my biggest supporters and cheerleaders would be a teacher. She was so beautiful and not like any other teacher. She certainly had her own style. I was in awe of her and how she taught and just how she was, as if we were all companions. She had a special essence. She may have been the first true Goddess who graced my life. Her impact remains with me to this day. I felt normal with her. She was always encouraging me and building me up. She was that one teacher who also felt like a friend. I could talk to her about anything. We did a lot of writing in her class, some of it in the form of short stories. One of the stories I wrote was about a "bird in a window." I will always remember Mrs. Neely saying to me, "Tammy, you are a great writer with huge potential. Whatever you do, never put your writing on the back burner. Tammy, keep writing, whatever you do, keep writing." Even though I did put my writing aside for over 30 years, her words are still etched on my heart and in my mind.

My senior year ended up being anything but ordinary. I was planning a wedding while everyone else was planning their graduation.

It was the natural thing for us to get married. That was the mindset in the area and in those the times. Pregnant and married went hand-in-hand. Tim never officially proposed to me. It was assumed by all of us that since I was pregnant, we would get married. The date was set, January 26, 1980. We were to get married in a Catholic church in Munjor, Kansas.

Not knowing the first thing about planning a wedding, I relied on Tim's mom, Natalie, to help me. Thank goodness Tim's mom and dad were right there for both of us, and not just with the wedding. They also helped us out by buying a lot to put a house on in the small town of Munjor, just down the street from where they lived. And they helped us find a used trailer house to move onto the lot.

I don't know what I would have done without Natalie to help me. I had no idea where to go shop for a wedding dress or how to go about it. I didn't have a car that worked. I relied on Tim and his pickup, which only got eight miles to the gallon so we didn't drive it all over the place. It was not like it is these days. You shopped local. You didn't get in your car and drive to the nearest city, which was about 90 miles away, to go wedding dress shopping. I was starting to show, so my dress options were minimal. It was a "fast" wedding, as people called it back then. When you said that term, everyone knew what you were talking about: the bride was pregnant.

Surprisingly, my dad was pretty stoked about the wedding. It was going to be one big happy party for him, and he invited everyone he had ever known through his business and personal life. Almost 400 invitations went out, and even though there was a major snowstorm the day before, about 350 people showed up.

I had so many mixed feelings about the event, and it didn't help that some family members were supportive and others were really pissed off at me. Sally, my dad's wife, was angry because their trip to Germany had to be postponed so Dad would have the money to pay for my wedding. Yet, then, she would complain to Dad that I was not involving her in the wedding plans. Hello, "Duh!" So to keep the peace, I invited Sally to come along to shop for wedding dress. Knock knock, hello. It was Dad who wanted the big shindig, not me.

My mom was not involved with my wedding, the plans or any of it. She was not sure where the "fine line" was and she was not paying for any of it. And, since Sally was helping my dad to raise me now, she felt she should bow out of the "mother of the bride" position. But, she was my mom, not Sally. It is odd how people perceive things.

Now that Wanda knew I was going to be her sister-in-law, she started to warm back up to me. Who knows what the issue really had been months before, maybe just something she had to work through. Together, Brenda, Wanda and Bonnie, my other bridesmaid, helped me out as much as possible.

I not only fell in love with Tim but also fell in love as much if not more with his family. His mom and dad were still together, something that I had lost when my mom and dad divorced. He had two different grandmothers and a really cool grandfather. Tim and I would go to his grandparents' farm on the weekends to visit and work when needed. I would go with his mom, Natalie, to visit his other grandmother. I started to feel as if I was in a real family again, something I never felt living with Dad and Sally. Tim's mom showed me how to do small quilting projects, which I really enjoyed. It was clear that family meant everything to her.

No matter how dark parts of our lives can be, there is always someone there. Sometimes they are right in front of you. Sometimes it can be hard to see them. It can be someone that you least expect. When despair grabs hold of you, do whatever it takes to reach out and ask for help, to anyone around you, to the person you least expect. When you think, "I do not want to bother them," *that is when you really need to make the call.* When you allow another person to help you, you are actually giving them a gift. The best parts of them are coming forth, their worthiness is deepening, and you are helping them to shine brightly. Think about it, how do you feel when you have helped someone over a hump in life? I bet like a million bucks, right?

I know that is how I felt after I worked with one of my clients, we will call him George. The morning after a coaching session with me, George and I had a check-in and what he told me blew my socks off. "How you doing George?" I asked over the phone. "Tammy, I took the bullet out of my pocket, the bullet I have had in my pocket for almost four months, wondering when I was going to use it on myself. Tammy, I took the bullet out of my pocket and feel like living again." Wow, I had no idea I was helping to save someone's life.

That is the gift you give to another when you reach out. This thought may be the catalyst you need when you are in a dark place, a place of depression, guilt, shame, the unknown, not understanding why you are feeling what you are feeling. I know, I have been through it all and then some. Maybe the thought that when you reach out for help from another, you are really giving them a gift and not bothering them, will encourage you to do ask for help. I pray that it encourages you to do so. I repeat: you are not bothering anyone. Reach Out. Ask for help.

CHAPTER 3
My Wedding Night

Obviously six months pregnant as I walked down the isle, was never how I thought my wedding day would be. Tim and I had a big wedding. That was his family tradition, his German heritage, so between that and my dad inviting everyone he knew, there were a lot of people there. On the day before our wedding, which was on January 26, 1980, there was a major snowstorm, so I was shocked when more than 350 guests showed up. We married in the St. Francis Catholic Church in Munjor, because that was Tim's family's church. Neither Tim nor I liked the priest, but we didn't have the option to choose a different one to marry us. Back then I would have been afraid of going to hell if I said we thought the priest was an arrogant prick.

Starting early in morning and going into the wee hours, the day was a full-on celebration. Pride of place was the big German meal — you've got to have the noodles, oh yes, those noodles at a wedding dinner. Dancing the night away was always a part of the festivities.

The continued support from Tim's family made me feel like I was getting a family that I didn't have, the family I always dreamed of having. It went beyond his mom and dad. Grandma and Grandpa Schumacher were also thrilled to have me in their family. Because Tim had been such a shy person growing up, and because I was his first girlfriend at the ripe old age of 20, his grandmother told me she was so happy that he found himself a girl. I still crack up laughing thinking about this.

Going to his grandma and grandpa's pretty much every weekend brought back some really great memories of going to my own grandmother's home as a child. Grandma took me under her wing and taught me how to bake some of her specialties, such as bierocks, sweet dinner rolls stuffed with ground beef, and cabbage, spiced just right. Yes, I can say I have carried on that tradition very well.

As I sit here and write this, I wonder why didn't I go see my grandmother and share times like this with her when I was an adult. I loved her so much, yet I did not make a point of going to see her and spending time with her. Driving those 40 minutes to Otis seemed like a major deal back then, and with being newly married and a new mother, I wondered if would it be ok with my husband. I assumed I had to ask permission, instead of making a statement and just going. My mindset was like that in many ways in those days.

We didn't have a honeymoon, not even years later. That was never even thought about or an option for us — with me being six months pregnant and having no job. Our income was solely dependent upon Tim, who made very little at the time. The next best thing was going to the local Holiday Inn to make our wedding night be somewhat special. The honeymoon was just another step in the process of marriage and living life together that many people take but was missing in our case. As mentioned, there was never a proposal. It was just assumed that we'd get married because I was pregnant. I wonder at times if it is weird that I still want him to ask me. Is that a girl thing? We bought the cheapest wedding ring we could find. Years later, after I fell and smashed my fingers, which required cutting my ring off, we never replaced it.

After a full day and evening of celebrating, we left the festivities early, even though people were still there hanging out and having fun. Arriving at the Holiday Inn, there was no "carry her over the threshold." Hmm, I wonder if they still do that these days? There was no romance, no hanky panky, no play time, nothing at all of the fantasy wedding nights portrayed in movies and books. Was it because we were both tired? Is that why I was so sad? Is that why I lay there, tears rolling down the sides of my face, as I did all I could to muffle my crying. Crying — I was in tears on my wedding night. Tim turned over on his side, his back to me, and fell sound asleep. I felt so sad and alone, even though my new husband was lying right beside me.

As I lay there, the floodgates opened more and more, as these thoughts were rolling around in my head: "What did I do? What did I just do? Tammy, what did you do?" Over and over these words kept playing in my brain. Then all of a sudden, this voice came to me and said with a sternness, "You made your bed, now lie in it!"

Whose voice was that? Was it God's voice? No it couldn't be, could it? God loved me more than that. God wouldn't talk to me that way, would He? Maybe He would. I grew up going to the local Baptist church, hearing about Hell and damnation and feeling I never measured up or was loveable enough. Was this programming inside of me, was that where the voice was coming from? I was so terrified of going to Hell when I was young that I made sure I was "saved" four times. As a young girl I remember thinking, "Oh maybe the last time didn't take, I better get saved again." To this day I am still deprogramming the religious teachings I learned so long ago, especially those based in so much fear, and I continue on a path of opening up to a higher way of thinking and new beliefs based in the Love of God.

As I lay there in these feelings of uncertainty, I needed to be held, I needed to share what was going on inside of me, I needed to be heard and be told everything was going to be okay, and that we are going to make it through this. I was scared, and there was my husband lying next to me oblivious to what I was feeling. I was trying to muffle the sounds of my crying, but I felt that he should have still have had some clue I was not a happy newly married bride. He should have known, right? That was my thought.

I did not wake Tim up. I didn't ask him to comfort me. How could he have known what was going on inside of me? We were married now, he was supposed to be able to read my mind. He was supposed to know. That is what the love stories in movies and books s always conveyed. I didn't ask him for help. At the age of 17, would I have known to ask for help? Tim never knew about the tears on our wedding night. I didn't tell him. I was too afraid of looking weak. Actually, it was more than that. Since I'd been pretty much on my own for years, I felt that I had to be strong and figure this out on my own. I'd had to figure things out on my own from such an early age, that it was ingrained in me at. That was what I was used to. What Tim needed from me was to tell him what was going on inside of me. Maybe I was also too afraid I would hurt his feelings. I was also used to looking out for other's feelings before mine.

Tim and I really didn't know how to communicate, especially when it came to serious stuff. We were so young. We were now married, not just dating anymore. There was so much confusion at that time in my life. We didn't have a chance to grow into an adult relationship. We went from being kids to being pregnant. I went from my dad's home to my husband's home. This may sound strange, but I didn't even know how I was supposed to dress. I was a teenager, yet I was a soon-to-be mom. I went to garage sales to get clothes because I had only a few outfits. What I bought was the old type of double knit pants and tops. I was supposed to dress like a mom, right? That is what they wore back then. What was I supposed to cook, and how do I cook it? It wasn't something I grew up learning. I was too busy out working to pay for my basic needs.

It's ok to have these confused and lonely feelings, and as mentioned in the last chapter, it is ok to ask for help. Actually it is vital to our very being, especially, when we feel lost and alone. I realized years ago that when I ask someone else for help, when I am vulnerable like that, showing the other person that I am not strong in the moment, I am giving them a gift. The greatest part of them, their gifts, can come forth when they help me. They receive validation and possibly even a knowingness of what they came here to be and do. They feel the importance of helping another human being. I have learned this practice but often have to remind myself that when I desire help, and the thought comes, "Oh, I don't want to bother them," that is when I call. That is when I get out of my mind and into my heart and reach out and ask for help.

What about the opposite? Are you paying attention to what those around you are need? Other people also look to you for help. But you do not have to be strong all the time. In a true relationship, you take turns being strong. You only have to be strong when the other person is weak. It is about listening to one another, listening with your ears and your heart. Be fully there with them, no distractions. In this way the person sharing is feeling fully validated, safe and secure as they become more raw and real in the moments of sharing.

I learned one lesson in asking for help from others in the summer of 2004 while attending an intense personal growth event over five days up in the mountains of Canada. It is not always with words that we ask for help; it can be with our eyes. Have you ever noticed that some people you come into contact with have an issue with allowing you to look into their eyes? I was that person for the first couple of days during that event. I kept my sunglasses on as I didn't want anyone to see my tears, and I didn't want to draw attention to myself. I was the strong one, always the strong one. Then, as I was sitting in silence, I heard this voice say to me, "Take off your sunglasses, Tammy, take them off. Allow others to see your pain." I was thinking to myself, "hell no!" Yet, I knew this was God whispering to my soul. I removed my sunglasses and kept them off, and wow, the love that shone from everyone who saw the pain in my eyes was overflowing. It was a new type of healing and brought a new level of understanding of the power of being vulnerable with others. It showed me a new way of being with other people.

Showing my vulnerability was terrifying at first, yet walking through that fear of showing my true self taught me that I would be accepted. It started to build trust with other people and gave me a level of safety. It means that when the tough times come around in a relationship, you'll be able to handle them much better. Start building in the good times and the not-so-bad times to be even stronger in your relationship with yourself, your spouse, and your other close relationships.

Are you aware of what those around you need? I have learned more and more how to do this. I have learned that we all have a love language. Although we think we are showing love to the other person, it does not mean that they are getting it. We may not be talking in their love language.

Let me share an example with you that has proven to be vital in my relationship with my husband. Tim and I both have the same love language — acts of service, but this does not mean that the same acts of service touch each of our hearts and souls. For instance, Tim gets really filled up when he sees me feed the cattle, or when I go along when he goes to check the livestock, or when I am helping him on a project. I have to think about what would fill him up. His acts of service for me are helping me with housework, taking me to a movie, or giving me flowers randomly. Helping me clean out the fridge turned out to be a major aphrodisiac for me. Ha, ha, ha. That really made Tim confused, but he enjoyed the rewards of helping.

It can be frustrating as you start to try and figure this out. First and foremost you must figure out your own love language. It will help so much in knowing what your own needs and desires are and why they are not being met, on any level. Keep with this work; it really pays off in aces.

CHAPTER 4

New Life

My baby, my baby! With tears still streaming down my face, my mind raced to my baby. I was doing what it took to protect the baby inside of me. I prayed, "I don't care what is wrong or right, help me make it through the night. I am going to do whatever it takes to make sure this baby has two parents." I was very determined for someone of such a young age. Some might say I am stubborn. I guess I had to be, to make sure this baby was going to grow up with mom and dad, both in the same house from the very beginning of its life.

That determination stemmed from remembering my dad talking scornfully of children born out of wedlock, kids born to single moms. There was a stigma around that when I was growing up that went back generations. It may be hard to understand this now, when it is accepted as how life just may be.

You were supposed to feel shame if you were pregnant before marriage, especially if you were on your own to have the baby, the dad not being in the picture. It was so bad with some parents, that if their daughter showed up pregnant, say in high school, the girl would be shipped off to a special "home" to have their baby. Or she was sent to a family member who lived in a town far away. The girl would have her baby and give it up for adoption, then go back to school the following year as if nothing ever happened.

The stigma was not only put on the unwed mother but also the baby. That precious baby was already shamed before being born. Through this backward mentality, this child, once gracing the earth with its presence, would carry that blame and shame even though it was not their fault. I didn't know until years later that my grandmother had been one of those unwed mothers when she was pregnant with my dad. I cannot imagine what that was like for her. I wish now that I had asked her more about that time in her life.

There was no way in hell my child was going to go through that. There was no way my baby was going to have to carry that stigma. I would do whatever it took to make sure that never happened. My baby was going to have two parents, and my baby was going to know what it was like to grow up being loved, to know it on such a level that he would never doubt it. That night I made that solemn promise to my child.

My children to come afterwards would also know without a doubt that they were loved. I knew what it was like to grow up feeling unloved and unwanted, wishing and praying with every single cell of my being that I could have parents that loved me. I am not saying my parents didn't love me. I am saying that is what I felt growing up, that I must have been unlovable. I would ask this question over and over: "Why do mommy and daddy not love me?" I knew the pain of a young child having those thoughts, feeling that distress. I would stand in my bedroom looking out the window at night hoping I was adopted. And I would pray so hard that my real parents would come and take me to my real home and love me very much and they would be so happy that I was with them.

I was determined to make sure that no child of mine would ever feel that. Somehow I would figure it out. I didn't know how, but in the end it came naturally to me. I was fortunate to be with a guy that felt as strongly about family as I did. I can see now that Tim was as scared as I was. However, I sure did not understand that 36 years ago when I was 17 and pregnant — with a woman's body and the mind of a teenager. In our own ways we were both committed to making sure our child would have two parents. That may partly explain the automatic assumption we would get married.

We may not have been rich, but our baby was going to have the best home ever. Yes, even if I had to hang out the cloth diapers in the middle of winter, my fingers freezing, being careful they did not get stuck on the metal clothesline. It was not about the things we could buy a child. It was about getting to grow up having the best childhood we could provide, knowing first and foremost that he is loved. Desiring to give my baby the very best start in life, I chose to breastfeed. Now, that was completely out of the norm. Everybody bottle-fed back then. I never allowed the odd looks that came my way to deter me from doing what I thought was best for my child, even though I was embarrassed at times. I had to figure that part out all on my own, because again I had no one in my personal life to help me sort this out. Thank goodness the one resource I did have was being able to call Dr. Myrick's office and talk to his nurse. She was kind and gentle with me, as she helped me through the fear and the tears when my left nipple was bleeding painfully and I wondered, "what am I doing wrong?" I am grateful that my daughters have organizations they can turn to if for some reason I cannot help them out in this area.

I felt so alone so much at that stage in my life, not sure of where to turn. My mom lived in a different town, living her own life and my sisters were not around. My friends were getting on with their lives, graduating, going to college, moving away. My stepmom was not there for me in any respect. Tim got a new job and was out of town a lot, or if not, was working long hours. Thank goodness I had my grandmother, although I didn't get to visit her much. But the few times I did go see her, I knew everything was going to be ok. She was always my saving grace while I was growing up, my source of love. She was the reason I did feel some love growing up. She loved me like no one ever did. I knew it and felt it. She always had this gleam of joy in her eyes when she looked at me. Hmmm, that feels glorious to remember.

Although I had no clue what I was committing to, there was this inner power, inner strength, that knew I was going to take care of my baby no matter what. Possibly that powerful knowingness came from that part that I think is within us all when someone we love, someone we care about, is threatened, or we feel they are threatened. My protective shield was up around my baby. Nobody was going to mess with this mama bear. There is a saying, "Hell hath no fury like a woman scorned." Well I would say there is nothing like the 'fury' within when this mom is making sure her baby is safe and loved.

To this day I am still astonished at Dr. Hull suggesting I have an abortion. To me he was telling me to kill my baby. Maybe that was why I was even more protective than the average mother. Yet, I am even more astonished and grateful of that the internal something, that mama bear in me that gave me the power to walk out of his office with such determination that no one was going to harm my child. I wonder sometimes what kept me from kicking him in the nuts and slapping him across the face before I walked out.

Being a parent, a real and true parent, takes commitment and it takes sacrifices. Almost anyone can have a baby but that does not mean you are a parent. It is about growing yourself to be better so you can be better for your child. Being a parent means allowing your child to grow into what they truly desire to be, not what you want them to be. I see so many parents who are trying to re-live their childhood through their children and then getting mad at their children when they do not meet the parents' expectations. This is so unfair to the child. It literally strips away their own identity and what they came here to be and do in the world. The child grows up thinking if they are not all that mom and dad want them to be then they do not matter. I know this personally — thinking I did not matter and becoming suicidal at the age of 14.

We are not here to live vicariously through our children. Make whatever you want happen in your own life. Do not put that burden on your child. Look within and figure your own stuff out. Do not make your child grow up before they are ready. Allow your children to have a childhood, have fun, play games. Inspire their imagination. Encourage their dreams to become reality no matter how far-fetched those dreams may seem to you. We as parents and guardians, as people who are in positions to highly influence children need to stop and think and understand the direction each child needs. It is not the physical things that matter. What truly matters is what is inside the child and how we can nurture and bring their gifts to the forefront, to help them expand and develop. This is true especially when it does not make sense for us and when that idea makes your child shine brighter than the sun.

Once a child knows, and really feels, they are loved unconditionally and feels safe in that love, wow, the limits are off. Their greatness starts to float to the top. One child may grow to be an amazing soccer player, while another is a social worker, and another is a stay-at-home mom. Whatever they end up choosing to be, allow them the privilege to make that decision for themselves — not something you desire so you can look good as their parent.

One of the ways I allowed my children's gifts to come forth is that I encouraged them to speak up and speak out, say what was on their mind without fear of being condemned or slapped across the face. I did have to call them on their tone of voice at times, and then they were allowed to repeat what they wanted to say, even to the point of telling me I was being bitchy. I never took it personally, even when they said the words most parents cannot bear to hear, "I hate you, Mom." When they would say that to me, I would smile and say, "That's ok, I still love you!"

The commitment to love, to being a mom, has been a continual journey and an unveiling of the greatest things in life. Staying with the choice of being a mom was not always easy. I had some really tough times along the way. Some of my own personal stuff would surface — the loneliness, the depression. But even with all the uncertainties of being a teenage mom and growing into a mom of five children, earning over 200 mom years, there remained this unyielding force within that knew I was here to teach my children. I was their teacher, not their best friend. What a disservice parents do to their children when they make their child their best friend as they are growing up.

Somehow, somewhere along the way, I knew God and Mother Mary were with me, helping to raise my children. Was it because I was committed to love, I was committed to making sure they grew up knowing in the deepest part of them that they were loved no matter what? I had this internal knowing that I was supposed to allow my children freedom, freedom to be themselves, allowing for mistakes to happen with their decisions. When they would fall from decisions not working out they would have a soft place to land. They had their home and it was built on the foundation of love.

CHAPTER 5

Joey

It is funny how our minds work — well, how mine worked back then, at such a young age and not knowing much about anything. I was really paranoid that I would not have a healthy child, like wondering if I had damaged him by smoking pot a couple of times before I had met Tim. What about the aspirin I took or the whiskey I drank? I kept wondering whether I could have damaged my baby. What else did I do, did I take any medicine? I would rack my brain trying to figure out what all I may have done to compromise my baby's health.

I wanted my baby boy to be so healthy that I would eat every single lunch at school. That is where part of my paycheck went. I made sure I had the money to pay for my lunch ticket, so I knew I would be getting a good meal that day. I would even go back up for seconds. I ate so much that I gained over 40 pounds during that pregnancy. Somehow I associated eating everything with a healthy baby. Even though I can laugh about it now and how silly that seems, it was not funny back then. I didn't know any better and had no one to advise me. I was on my own to figure out my pregnancy and motherhood.

That was all I knew at that time in my life. That is how I grew up, doing the best I could with no one to turn to, no one in my immediate family. I followed the direction of Dr. Myrick, the doctor I found on my own. I felt completely safe with Dr. Myrick, knowing he would take the best care of my baby and me. He was always open to answering my questions, and more importantly, he never, ever judged me. That was extremely important to me, as a teen and pregnant. He was the kindest and most wonderful doctor I have ever known.

I still remember what he said after the birth of my fourth child, Jenna, about how miraculous that whole experience had been. Dr. Myrick looked at me with tears of wonder in his eyes and said, "Tammy, you never cease to amaze me, your births are so unique and different. I need to write a book about you." Dr. Myrick was a saving grace for me at that time in my life. I was fortunate that he was the doctor for all of my five children.

With my due date approaching, Tim and I went to Lamaze training. I learned the different ways to breathe for the different stages of delivering a baby. We attended six classes to prepare us for the birth of our first child. My belly was really big by that time.

On Mother's Day, 1980, Tim and I got ready to go to town. We were meeting at my dad's house to go to the Farm and Home Show with Dad and Sally, and Tim's parents, Marion and Natalie. I was feeling weird and thought I was coming down with the flu. I told Tim I thought I was going to be sick so we went back home and I lay down to take a nap. Well, I tried anyway, but I was really uncomfortable. My back hurt, and I was feeling constipated. I had no idea that this is a sign of being in labor.

Still oblivious as to what was actually going on with me, I told Tim to take me to the hospital, as I knew something was not quite right. Upon arriving at the hospital, I was admitted and found out I was dilated. Tim and I looked at each other in shock. Um, oh, we are going to have a baby. The nurses said, "You are only dilated to three, but since we are not busy we will keep you." It's a good thing they did because within an hour I doubled that and shocked the nurses in the process.

Even though Tim and I had done what we could to prepare for the birth by going to Lamaze classes, in the moment when it actually happened that training went out the window for a bit. As we began to get comfortable in the labor room, Tim sat there with the TV on. It didn't take long before a contraction came on and I started yelling at him, "Turn that damn TV off and help me breathe!" Tim turned off the TV, and came to stand by me, and did the best he could. We were there in the labor room, the two of us, scared, not sure of what was happening, how it was going to happen, by ourselves trying to figure it out, breathing through the contractions.

Soon, I was ready to go to the delivery room. Thirty-six years ago, there were two rooms for birthing a baby, a labor room where you stayed until the last minute, then, when the timing was right, you were wheeled into the delivery room. It was a surgical room of some sort, with all the equipment, needles and so on that might be needed.

The nurses must have thought I was crazy, because as soon as I was laid up on the delivery table and a contraction came I started screaming through it. I hadn't done that in the labor room, but in the delivery room it seemed natural to add in the screams. That is what we all were taught since early in life by the movies and TV shows we watched — the women always screamed when they were giving birth. They also sometimes cussed out loud.

The nurse that soon became my favorite was Sue Spier. All it took was for me to scream one time, and Sue walked over to my side, looked straight into my eyes and said, "Tammy did you take Lamaze?" I said, "yes" and Sue said to me, "Then find your focal point and *breathe*, there is no need to be screaming, find your focal point and breathe!" Her firm, yet loving tone was all I needed. Bam, all those thoughts of screaming went right out of head, and the Lamaze training came flooding back. I never screamed again.

"Come on Tammy just one more push, just one more push. You got this girl, you got this." The team of nurses and the doctor were cheering me on. Tim was standing beside me the whole time, doing his best to help me through this. Relief soon happened for a brief moment as our baby boy, Joseph Lee Schumacher, made his entrance into the world, only three hours after I arrived at the hospital. The nurses were very excited and in shocked amazement at our baby. They were telling me what a good job I did, and they started to bet each other on how much he weighed.

"Wow, over a nine-pound baby, he has to be at least nine pounds." They were going back and forth on how much they were guessing his weight at. I heard this gasp from one of the nurses and asked, "what's wrong," as they laid Joey in my arms. "Nothing is wrong, Tammy, you have a very healthy 10 pound, 6 ounce baby boy." I did not know that that was a pretty huge baby to have, especially your first time, and for me to deliver completely normally, no drugs were involved, was pretty outstanding. There was no way I was going to have anything. Again, I was making sure my baby was going to be healthy, so I chose to have a completely natural birth, as natural as you can get when having a baby in the hospital.

A woman only dilates to 10 cm and Joey's head was 14 cm. Needless to say, many stitches were required. Then, I was saying yes to anesthesia, and I sure let the doctor know when it was not working as he was stitching me back up.

We had a baby, now what? What are the next steps? Even though I took full responsibility for my child, that did not mean I knew how to do things. I had my baby on Mother's Day, but I was feeling a bit lost on to where to go from there. I had my baby, and I had to figure this out on my own. No one was there to give me advice.

Tim went back to work the day after I had Joey, because it was a Monday. He came to see me in the hospital when he got off work. He was just starting a new job. Do you dare ask to take off time to be with your wife and new child? Neither one of us thought of that in those days. Do you really ask a favor like that?

When I got released from the hospital, it was Tim's mom who picked me up to bring me home. It was not Tim and me as a couple bringing our baby home for the first time. It was Tim's mom who took me to the store to get things before taking me home.

I never realized in the moment of Tim not taking me home that it would cause issues for me down the road. Later I wondered why he did not care enough about me and our newborn child to be the one to pick us up. I know he was working. However, looking back as I did over time, I thought we should have asked the doctor to release me in the evening, when Tim could have been the one to come and get me. These thoughts started to weigh on me, and feeling that he did not care about me — feelings layering on top of one another that he did not really care. If he did care, he would have known better. That's was what was in my mind, that he was supposed to know.

Hindsight is 20/20. The understanding I have now helps me to see that Tim was trying to earn a living for me, his new wife, and our new baby. Maybe he was too scared to rock the boat at his new job. This makes so much sense now, understanding why it was Natalie who brought me home from the hospital. Back then there was not even the thought, as there is today, that the dad takes time off to be with his newborn baby and his wife. That was beyond any realm of thinking.

We can prepare all we need to for that one time when we really need the training and then it can fail us. In the heat of the battle, in the moment when we need it most, our training may be nowhere to be found. I prepared for the birth by learning Lamaze. I knew all the breathing techniques, I practiced them. Yet, when it came to the very moments when I required them, the old programming that I grew up with, the screaming in childbirth was so real to me that it took over. The right person needed come to me and shake that old thinking out of me, so that I could focus on what I had learned.

Tim was there, but he was not a coach, one that was firm enough to get me on the right path. He was as unsure of himself as I was. Someone else had to come into the mix and help me to see what I was and was not doing and how to continue down the appropriate path — the path of breathing through childbirth and no longer screaming. Learning that was a pivotal point in my life. I was empowered, even though I did not know that word back then. I knew I could handle giving birth to my baby.

There are times when we have to reach out to people beyond our normal circle. Sometimes we require that extra helping hand to bring a new awareness. Sometimes someone else can help us see where to make the improvement we need.

There are strong people like Nurse Sue, and we need them in our lives, especially if you are like me and desire to continually grow and become more tomorrow than you are today. We need people who have our best interest at heart; that person may be a coach, a friend, a mentor, a teacher — whoever can help you to see your value and your gifts, especially when you cannot. This is a part of what I do for and with my coaching clients. I am thrilled when the light turns on in their mind and their heart.

Sometimes we need a person who has the ability to help us to see when we are veering off the track of who we came here to be. You know the one, the one that you trust so much, that you know they will set you straight if you require it. Just like nurse Sue did with me. That is the only type of people that I allow in my inner circle these days — my no-filter, say-it-like-it-is, friends.

Our precious baby boy, our little Joey, our perfect healthy little baby with a big head, ha ha ha, our blessing, our future, our grace. How did we get so lucky? Thank-you, God!

CHAPTER 6

Pregnant Teen

I no longer had a job. I had been working for a while at JCPenney, until they found out I was pregnant, a teen pregnant. They fired me, or more accurately, they just took me off the schedule. The manager at that time was too much of a chicken to tell me I was fired. I showed up to work according to the original schedule and people looked at me weird, and then I found out that my name had been removed from the roster. No one even told me. When I asked what was going on, a co-worker told me I no longer worked there. I didn't know enough at the age of 17 to pursue it any further.

At that time Tim was being paid less than minimum wage at his job. He loved working there, even though he had to work six days a week. He liked his boss and most of the people who came into the gas station. They had a great hard worker in Tim, and yet they did not appreciate him enough to pay him what he was worth. Tim found a better job, and that relieved some of our stress — better pay was on the horizon. We were very glad that Tim started a new job in April 1980, a month before our first child was due to arrive. Our only income was the paycheck that Tim brought home.

Even though it felt strange having a baby shower while I was still a senior in high school, I was grateful for the gifts I received. I had no idea how we were going to afford all of the necessities for raising a baby. However, even at my young age and even though I was scared at times, I always felt God would be there by my side helping me along.

The one thing we were not prepared for though, with Tim's new job, was the fact that he would still work long hours, and when he wasn't at his job he would be working at the farm at night after his job. During the weekends he would also be up at the farm with his dad and grandparents, helping them out, making sure that things were maintained and fields were worked and that all things that come with farming got done. He was his dad's right hand. It was expected of him. There was never an option to say "no." It was understood: Tim would be there to help out.

As a result, there was no time for our relationship to be nourished and to blossom. This is not the way it was supposed to be, this was not what TV portrayed, this was not how marriage and having a family and the "loving" couple with the gleam in their eyes were supposed to be living. TV and magazines had tricked me into believing the fairy tale. We were thrust into adulthood and parenthood in one large swoop, and in a family that never talked about their emotions, wants or needs.

When Tim was home, he was so exhausted from all the hard work he did, there was not much if any left over for "us." So, if I wanted to be with him, for the little bit he would take a break to come in and eat, or for those brief snatches of time in between farm jobs. I would choose to go to the farm and hang out, while Tim was again off and working, this time out and about with his dad and grandpa. I might see him for brief snatches of time in between farm jobs.

I felt an isolation like I had never imagined living in the small town of Munjor, about 10 minutes away from Hays, where I grew up. We didn't have much money starting out and our pickup was a gas hog. That pickup was Tim's pride and joy, so much so that 36 years later Tim still has his 1973 GMC 4 x 4 blue and white two-ton truck.

There were no friends to come to see me. They were going their own way with graduation coming up. My mom lived in a different town, not that far away but she did not really care to come and see me. My sisters were doing their own thing in their own lives, and anyway we never were really all that close growing up. And my dad and his wife were living their own life. I felt like I had fallen off the face of the earth. All I had was Tim's family. I felt stuck, abandoned, isolated and alone. Where were all the people in my life who said they cared about me, who said they loved me? Where the hell were they?

By March of my senior year, I had earned all my credits to officially graduate and no longer had to attend classes. I thought, "I am done, but what do I do now?" I felt like I was forgotten. I was out of the picture. I didn't finish out the year in the classrooms. It was an odd feeling to no longer be required to go to school and not being around my friends, just staying at home all day, for the first time, being by myself, no job, waiting for my baby to come.

Then I found out that I would be allowed to walk across the stage with all my classmates to graduate. Even though it was too late to order the same gown everyone else had, Tim and his mom helped me to come up with the idea of wearing Tim's graduation gown. It did not matter to me that it was not the right length and had faded over the years hanging in his closet. At this graduation ceremony, 10 short days after I gave birth to our son Joey, I would be walking across the stage with the rest of my classmates, faded gown and hat. I didn't care. I was determined. I had thought it was not an option and then this opportunity opened up for me. I was going to make sure it happened. It was a proud moment for me.

Tim's mom and dad, Natalie and Marion, included me in all the festivities of the event. They treated me as if I was their own daughter. There was a party at their home, and I was celebrated along with Wanda, Tim's sister, both of us walking across the stage that day.

Is this all there is to life? What am I doing? What is my purpose? What does my future hold? I started asking these questions at the age of 17. There had to be more to this thing called life. Home alone with a baby on the way, not knowing much at all, not even knowing how to really cook, making my new husband mad because of the meals I attempted to cook, yet was not good at, feeling like a failure in that area of our life. I was learning one step at a time how to take care of a house, a baby, a husband, feeling lost and alone and on my own to figure it all out. The washer not working right, the sewer backing up into the tub in the other bathroom.

At times in my life, when I have felt I was the forgotten one, somebody reached out and pulled me back — like Brenda letting me know that I could graduate with the class I had been with for over four years. There are people in your midst too. Sometimes they are hidden from us in the pain of what we are experiencing in the moment and then they come forth. Somehow they hear our cries for help, for understanding. Is this the Divine sending its Earth Angels to help us out? That is what I believe. This was not the only instance when someone came along and brought me back into the picture.

This time it was Brenda. She was the reason why I walked across the stage and received my diploma. She reached out to me to tell me; she pulled me back in to the graduation event.

Accepting my diploma in person was pretty damned exciting. It made me see that even if I was mistake to some people, being a senior and having a baby, that it did not make any difference. I no longer felt alone or like a misfit. I had sunk my flag into the ground, and no matter what happened in life, I still made a goal to come through for me. Now this part of my life was complete and I could move more whole into my new life.

The mind is powerful, and it can lead us on a downward spiral when we are in difficult times. The mind can play tricks on us. Beware when you feel that loss, that aloneness, that confusion, of where your mind leads you if you allow yourself to keep going down the "why" path — asking the "why" questions. Why Me? Why this? Why, why, why?

Instead of asking "why," ask, "How can I make this better?" When you ask that question, you start to see the possibilities of answers, of ways out of the why. You start to take responsibility for where you are at and how you got there. Then you take control of the situation and start to pull yourself up and out of the why and into the how and the now.

This is all about attitude. Asking "why" sounds like whining, and you get nowhere fast with that mindset. Asking "how" opens you up to new awareness and answers that have been waiting for you to ask so they can flow to you. When we get that downward spiral going we can talk ourselves into anything, and we have the capability to make it darker and darker and darker, especially when we are all alone.

We all need someone. No one is an island. We need friends, someone who looks out for us to some degree, someone who will give us a shake once in awhile. We need a network, a village. For me, that was Brenda for a bit, and there were Tim's folks. They made sure I was a part of the family. Tim's mom taught me a little bit of how to quilt and other things I never knew. I felt included sitting with her quilting a baby blanket for my son. In retrospect, I wish I had done more of that with Natalie, learned more with her, things like the quilting, creating more and being more consistent with it, not the one time baby quilt she helped me make for Joey. There are other lost skills that were something I could have handed down to my children and their children. I remember going to Grandma Josie's house, Natalie's mother, the quilt was laid out on this big rack and we hand-quilted it together, the three of us.

Depending on how far down the spiral we may be, seeing the help that is within our reach may be elusive to us. We need to be aware of not being alone, to reach out to someone, anyone, especially when we feel ourselves going into a downward spiral, because that is a lonely place to be.

Determination is a requirement in life, to stay on task and fight for our goals. Take, for example, the determination I had to get my credits completed well before my due date. I could have said, "I am dropping out. I am going to be a mom anyway." I stayed on task, even with all these other feelings and thoughts and judgements that kept coming to me, even when feeling lost and alone and really really out and on my own when it came to school. I got my credits done and I finished school. Digging deep inside is sometimes what we need to do to pull up that determination. We do what we do to make things happen.

CHAPTER 7

Look After Yourself First

hat is wrong with me? This is a question I was asking frequently by the time I was 21. I had two children by this time, Joey, and Crystal, born in the summer of 1983. I was married and we had moved in to a new home, yet I was not living the dream life as it was portrayed in the movies and TV shows. I wondered what was wrong with me. Why was I always crying, being so emotional at the smallest of things? Why were things just not working the way I always thought they would, being in love and having a family? Everything was not all hunky dory.

I knew I needed help, but I just was not sure how to go about it. Look in the Yellow Pages, I guess. I saw an ad for a mental health facility and I chose to go there.

It really was not all that long ago, 30 some years, but seeking counseling had a horrible stigma attached to it then. No one ever came out and said they were doing that. It was an attitude in the air. It was as if you were a person with leprosy, like they talked about in the Bible.

I didn't care though as I felt I was going crazy at times, and I knew I needed help. And who knows if it was post-partum depression, as they call it now, after having my second child. Something was again happening with me. I didn't know how else to help myself. The only thing I knew was traditional counseling. I was lucky enough that they charged on a sliding-scale. They went by our income, and since we were a one income family with two children, I was fortunate that I only got charged $11 an hour. This was the first of many times I was to search for counseling, for help, for guidance.

Tim's mom, Natalie, would watch the kids for me, that summer of 1983, when I would go to town, get groceries and take an hour to go see my counselor. I didn't tell her about the counseling part at first, and I didn't tell Tim either. I didn't know how to say to my husband, "Oh by the way, I started counseling." Really, that was not a choice for me. I felt I had to hide the fact that I was seeing someone to help me out, to help me understand what was going on with me.

Wow, I now had someone to listen to me with heart and soul. I really think that was part of it. At this point in my life, I had no one to talk to. No mom, she was living her own life. No dad, he was busy building his business and gallivanting around. No friends, they had all gone their own way. So finding a counselor who would listen to me and help me figure out my thoughts, sure did help. I started to feel happier about things, about life.

One night I drove into the driveway and Tim asked me where I was. With a timid voice I told him I was seeing a counselor and had come from an appointment. I was about six sessions in at this point. As I had been afraid of, he was pretty pissed, so much so that he ordered me to quit going, that he was not going to pay for me to go see a damned shrink, even if it only cost $11 a session. Being shocked and upset at how he reacted, I did quit going.

Looking back, I think it was really that he was more concerned about his own image. What would people think about him if his wife was going to see a shrink? What would people think about him as a man and a husband, that he couldn't control his wife better than that? Possibly the money excuse was just that, an excuse. He grew up in a household with everyone hiding their feelings, never talking about their feelings. In his family, you never let it out in public that you were having problems in your own life that you are soooo bad that you had to go see a shrink. People judged one another on that type of thing. That is why it was so hidden and why I was sneaky about it. It was the only way. There was an understanding that you never admitted out loud the difficulties you were having in your personal life, in your marriage. People would put on a show no matter how miserable they were. That was Tim's culture, how he grew up and lived around.

I was raised as a Baptist and had always had the Bible drilled into my mind, along with the guilt and the shame of never being good enough for God. I still remember that the wedding vow of Love, Honor and Obey thy Husband and that idea being preached by the pastor every Sunday from the time I was a young impressionable girl. Also there was the notion that where two are joined they become one. There was no equality, the woman was subservient to the man. That is what I saw and grew up with. My mom always put my dad's wants and needs ahead of everybody else's. I was always told I was second best, if that, that my dad would always be the most important one to her. I mentioned before how on Monday evenings, when dad was out of town, Mom, my sisters and I would watch *I Love Lucy*, all of us laughing so much. Yet, when dad was home on Monday nights it was never an option. We even got yelled at by Mom if we dared to ask Dad, because it started at the same time as Monday night football did. I grew up hating football mainly for that reason, as a little girl feeling football was more important to my dad and mom than I was.

The man was always the boss of the household when he was around. The men made the money, and they controlled the money. "Keep the woman barefoot and pregnant and at home" was the mindset. Who was I to speak up? I was just a stay-at-home mom, something that was not a very highly regarded profession at that time.

One time I asked Natalie, my mother in law, "Why don't you stick up for yourself? Why don't you say 'no,' or do it yourself? Why do you act like you are the maid?" She looked at me with a sad look on her face and told me, "That is just the way it is." I felt my heart sink, thinking, surely this is not the way it is supposed to be, this is not the way to live being a wife and mother.

After Joey and Crystal were born, Sally, my dad's second wife, made the comment to me that she wished she hadn't listened to my dad and had had more fun with my kids. Instead, she dressed as my dad wanted her to look, sophisticated and put together at all times. Sally told me that she knew she missed out by not playing on the ground or on the floor with my kids. She wished she would have put on jeans and roughed around with the kids. Sally made this comment to me shortly after playing a little ball with Joey out in the front yard of our house. Joey with his big fat plastic blue bat and Sally pitching that big fat plastic ball to him. Oh the smiles on both their faces, and on Joey's face when he hit that ball,. It was priceless. I am sure that is what made Sally think of the times she missed. She had really enjoyed herself playing with Joey like that.

It is our responsibility to take care of ourselves. When people depend on one another, to the extent of expecting that other person to take care of their needs, that is where the pain starts to come in. I did that. I depended on my husband Tim to make me happy. I grew up with the thought that it was his job, not mine, to do so. For instance, now, if I want flowers, I just go buy them for myself. I am no longer dependent on someone else to make me happy and content. I have even shocked different florists, one In particular, when he asked me who the bouquet was for, and I told him, "Me. I am buying it for me. His response was, "Wow, good for you, I wish more women would do that for themselves."

It is like the oxygen mask on a plane — you have to put it on yourself first and then help others. You can only help care for others if you take care of yourself first and foremost. I admit at times I have to remind myself of this as I do lose sight of this knowledge from time to time. In my own experience and as a result of conversations with other women, I believe this is where depression often stems from. When a woman depends on her man to take care of her wants, needs and desires, she will never be fulfilled.

Remember, women: people are who they are and do what they do. If your husband or partner is not the type to go buy you flowers and yet you expect him to know to do so, especially let's say for Valentines Day, you are setting yourself up for disappointment. In my opinion, it is upon me to make sure to get the flowers for myself. That way I cannot get upset when he does not show up with the flowers. The disappointment is less, and the pressure is off of the other person to perform to your expectations.

We start to gather this confidence within us on many levels. I knew I needed counseling, I needed help of some nature. I felt like I was breaking into pieces and my husband could not understand that. He thought it was easy to just stop it. It was not easy for me. Sometimes we just have to rock the boat in our relationships. I know some women that say they're happy, and act as if they are happy in their relationships, yet when they really get deep, when they wish to do this or that, they do not do it because they do not want to make their spouse upset, or they feel their spouse will not understand.

It is time to quit asking for permission. Your husband is not your father; he is your partner in life. I completely understand that he may not understand why, what or how you desire to do what you want to do, but let it be his problem. That is not for you to pull back on what you truly desire. For instance, let's say I am going on a trip to another country. I tell my husband, "I want to let you know I am going to Egypt in February of next year. Do you have any questions or thoughts?" I am to the point. I'm making a statement and sharing with him. I no longer ask for permission, like I did when we were first married, which opened up a whole different dialogue, one that allowed for me to be told "no." All that brought me was disappointment and heartache when he did not agree with me for any reason.

About 10 years into our marriage I "asked" about me going back to school. I wanted to attend college and get a degree, and the first thing that came out of my husband's mouth was, "I am not going to invest into something I do not see a return on." My hopes were dashed. I never mentioned it again, even though the desire was deep within me.

How I wished I had had the courage to state what I wanted, go through with it, rock the boat and allow things to unfold however they would. I now know that if the other person has an issue, it is about them, not about me. We have to take a stand for ourselves. It is about bringing our power forth, to voice what is really inside of us, allowing those wishes and dreams to have a voice, to be realized and come to fruition. Our needs and wishes depend on us to make them come true. Even though that is how society was at that time in life, I wish I would have had a strong female role model to help me understand that I was worth it. I was worthy of attending college, getting my degree and more, then and now.

Growing up, I was told more than once that my dad was number 1 to my mom. How well I remember Mom telling us girls, "Your father will always be number 1 to me. You girls never will. One day you will be gone and it will just be your dad and me. He will always be number 1."

I grew up thinking I was never number 1 with anybody. I can understand my mom thinking that, yet that is not what you tell your child, that they will never be number 1. Even though at the age of 13 my parents divorced, I still had the ingrained thought, "I will never be number 1." It is time, women, it is time that we become our number 1. We must take care of ourselves first. Allow the guilt of doing that to go away. Work through it and bring yourself up to a higher level. This is one of the main reasons I started my coaching practice, to assist women to rise to their full potential, to know that they matter, to heal the shame, pain and guilt and to give permission to be the number 1 that they are.

CHAPTER 8

Foundation Building

I was in my 20s and there were good times, just like in everyone's marriage. It was so wonderful at one point that we would often laugh and spend good times together when the two kids, Joey and Crystal, were in bed. It was such a special time that I remember the moment I got pregnant with our third child, Shanna. I felt we were so in love at the moment of her conception. There was this softness, the feeling of completeness of being a couple. I wanted so much to have more of these times.

Our first home was a three-bedroom used trailer home. It was ok. It was paid for and we had our own place. We didn't have it very long before Tim started thinking we should move to a different house. Actually we both did after the trailer got hit by a tornado. Thank goodness we were not at home. The winds were so strong that they moved the trailer off its foundation, and there was glass from the window was in Joey's bed. We were so fortunate to not be at home when it hit. During those times we were busy with life, Tim off at his job and afterwards up at the farm helping his dad and grandpa out.

We continued to weave in and out of different relationship levels, from being-in-love feelings and actions to being more like partners or roommates working on the physical level. I assumed that was just how marriages were. The fun and games of dating were over. We went from being kids, to being parents, to not knowing how to work out our relationship ups and downs. Tim would talk to his mom more than he would talk to me about our problems. His mom would relay to me what Tim was thinking, and I would think, "Why doesn't he tell me this, or that?"

We sold the trailer and moved a two-bedroom house onto a full cinder-block basement. That was the thing to do: move a house, not build it. Yeah, I know, a bit out there. Ha ha. I thought the same thing when his dad and Tim were talking about how to move the house and where to put it. This is something that I had never known about growing up, but apparently, that is how the house Tim grew up in came about. It was moved to the site. His dad and grandpa used to work with a guy that moved houses so it was normal for Tim and his family. For me it was outrageously cool how someone could move a house.

Once the house was moved, early in the summer of 1982, even though I was 8 months pregnant with Crystal, it did not stop me from working on things and getting things ready for our second baby to arrive. Tim and I started working together to get our home ready for our increasing family. It was an older house and required a lot of work to bring it up to modern standards. Tim was great at doing this type of thing as he grew up doing small construction jobs with his dad on their own home. Later, on the wintry days, with Tim at home from his job at decent hours, we worked at night after the kids were in bed and started putting up sheetrock and that kind of thing. We did what we could with limited funds to create a nicer home environment.

One day I was helping Tim carry sheetrock into the house from the garage and we hit a patch of ice. I went down hard but, wanting to protect the corners of the sheetrock and not to get Tim mad at me if I dropped it, I hung on to the sheet and severely smashed my fingers. My wedding ring was jammed very tight into my now swelling fingers. Tim was really concerned and did everything possible to cut my wedding ring off of my, what we thought was a broken finger. In moments like this, I knew he loved me. I knew it in my head, but for some reason it was not reaching my heart. There was no emotional level to connect with, none that I saw or felt. When I attempted to share my thoughts and feelings, I felt like I was talking to a brick wall. I even told him that at different times, saying, "The wall listens to me more than you do!"

I expected my husband to be my knight in shining armour. I guess that means I am a romantic at heart, and I thought my husband would be the same. Why wouldn't he be? He certainly was when we were dating, to the point that he bought a 350 Honda when he found out how much that I liked motorcycles. For my wants, needs and desires, Tim was not playing the roll that I expected, that I learned growing up husbands were supposed to do. I wanted to know I was adored and cherished by my husband. Instead I felt more like his maid. In the TV shows I had watched as a girl the man was always so excited to see his wife, shows like *Leave it to Beaver, Happy Days, Eight Is Enough, Little House on the Prairie, The Waltons*, and the list goes on. Not only was the husband in the show lovingly attentive to his wife, the husband and wife also had meaningful conversations. They discussed things, sometimes things pretty deep, like their feelings. Ever since I was a little girl I used to dream of being in the Walton Family. I wished so hard to have a Walton family.

All the hard work Tim did, and the sacrifices I made, were us working together to make sure I was able to be a stay-at-home mom, raising our children, which eventually would number five. We both agreed on that. In my mind then Tim was not only supposed to be bringing home the bacon, but to also to be bringing emotional stability to me. Instead I was experiencing an emotional roller coaster because he did not listen to me or help me at all. Rather than bringing any stability, he was adding to the roller coaster because I never knew what the hell he was thinking. There was no communication on the emotional level.

I spent so much time thinking. I was thinking about what did I do, what did I not do. I worried about all kinds of things that I might have done wrong, and I was second guessing myself instead of enjoying the moment and being in a positive place. If I had been enjoying what was going on, I think that would have moved me away from the depression. If I could have been in the moment and enjoying it, that probably would have taken away the darkness. I spent all this time second guessing and worrying over a non-existent future. I could have enjoyed even more times together with us and with our family. Tim didn't want me to use to dryer even in the winter months so we could save on the electricity bill, and so I listened and obeyed my husband's wishes. However, I eventually put my foot down. I was not freezing my fingers off anymore. There are some extremely and frigid temperatures here in Kansas. When I started using the dryer more and more, he really didn't say anything. Was I over being afraid of rocking the boat, or was he starting to recognize me and feel the courage that was growing inside of me to start standing my ground? I don't know.

We needed to know how to communicate, to hear each other. I know that is what I needed. I needed Tim to speak up and tell me what he needed. He expected me to know, to be like his mom, to have supper ready and on the table no later than 5:30 when he walked in the door from work. For years and years, I would ask Tim what was wrong when he was moody. I would beg him to talk to me and when he wouldn't, I would ask myself, "what did I do, what didn't I do, what did I say, what didn't I say?" I would literally drive myself into a depression, trying to figure out how to make my marriage work. I took on the whole responsibility of making things happen, of making things better. I felt I was walking on egg shells around him most of the time in those early years, not wanting him to go off on one of his unpredictable bursts of anger or frustration, not sure what to call it.

In our earlier years, when I did not understand that he was a meat and potatoes type of man and I made a breakfast meal for supper, he was so upset after I set his plate in front of him that he took his 44 ounce tomato beer and threw it at me. Standing there in utter shock, as our son Joey was sitting in his highchair nearby, with tomato beer dripping off of me, I immediately learned never to have breakfast as a supper meal ever again.

I did not always put Tim first like my mom did with my dad. Because I had grown up knowing I was second best, if that, my initial drive as a mother was to make certain my children knew without a doubt they were loved, cherished and adored.

We just didn't know better. We didn't know how to talk to each other. We didn't have tools to communicate with each other to the point of really hearing what the other person was saying and sharing.

In retrospect, I don't know whether I was overreacting, and maybe Tim was not as stingy and negative as I thought and feared. At the same time, when I started to dry the diapers in the dryer, maybe Tim realized that I was a strong person and was going to do the things that I wanted, so he decided to cut me some slack. Either way, I do know that we did not know how to communicate and that was what the real problem was at that time. We just didn't know.

We worked together to fix up the house, to create a home out of this house we moved into in our early years together, bringing ourselves up a few steps at a young age. We could work together physically and we worked well together. We were a bit more than partners of convenience. But we absolutely had to learn to communicate on that next level, not just which piece of sheetrock goes up next. We needed to discuss why we were building our dream. Being on the same track, through discussing our goals and our dreams, makes the journey so much easier and more enjoyable.

We did eventually start to build a dream together, to build a legacy. Going into our fourth year of marriage, and with our third child on the way, we started to think about our future together and actually purchased our first quarter of farm ground. It was Tim's dream that I went along with, wanting him to be happy. After four years of being married, we went against even the banker, who said, "There is no way this you are going to make this work out for you. You are not going to be able to make the payments." I think that pissed Tim off just enough that not only did we make all the payments on time, we also paid off that quarter of land early.

Tim's grandpa and his dad were surprised and pleasantly shocked at the drive that Tim and I had to make it happen, and I stood by him and encouraged him no matter what we were going through as I saw this was his dream. And soon after that we discussed how we were going to leave this land as a part of our legacy to our growing family. We started to discuss what we could build together.

We even gave the land a name. Joey and Crystal were bouncing up and down when they saw Tim and his dad, "Popo," getting ready to go check out this piece of land. The children kept saying, "I wanna go, I wanna go," over and over. Finally, their Popo looked down at them and said, "You can't go this time because we are going over to Booxstohooey." That meant they were going far far away, which actually made it more enticing for the kids.

We were seeing that the goals we had discussed here and there were starting to come to life. It was odd how I felt though. I never really understood it, but I always felt, even though we bought the land together and it was a mutual decision, that it was Tim's land. When we moved to the family farm over 30 years ago, it was Tim's farm. I never felt it was mine, or ours, not until major shifts and shakeups happened later in our marriage.

There were flashes of brilliance where it was a good relationship. Those didn't necessarily make it positive. Those good times sometimes made it worse because then I would wonder why it was not like that all the time. Those showed me that it could be better and I wondered why it couldn't be like that more of the time. Yet, those flashes of brilliance did give me the hope to keep on keeping on.

Times have changed. A lot of what I am sharing about my earlier years, that was the way things were done at then. It really was not that long ago when things started to change. I am 54 now, and I would say that it has only been in the last 25 years. Yet it was a slow, very slow, step-by-step process. I was stepping into unchartered territory, one where many women who I was around were not willing to go. So, many times, I felt alone on this journey.

I chose to intensify my process in April 2003 and have been going full-steam ahead ever since. It's maybe 15 years since things have started to take a turn to a more positive light. The times I am talking about almost seem medieval, as women and children were viewed as property. That is just the way things were done at that time. I was fortunate enough to choose, to take a leap and get a second start and live in more modern times. I fought hard for my second start. I started to see the different possibilities that were out there to be explored.

I know that fear of rocking the boat. I know that loneliness of being on a different path than those who are around me. I know the loss of the old, but also the welcoming and opening up to the new. Women: if you require permission, if you feel you need permission, I give you permission to begin your second start now. You can do it. I believe in you! It does not matter how old you are, whether you are older or younger than my 54 years. Start today. If I can do it, so can you!

CHAPTER 9

The Birthday

As I was approaching the turning 30 mark in my life, I didn't understand the many women who claimed they did not want to reach that age. And I saw how women close to me, one in particular reacted to turning 30 — crying, depressed, hating the fact that she was going to be so old. I committed to myself that when it was my turn, I was going to celebrate being 30. I was going to have fun. I was going to make it one of the best days of my life. The fact that this commitment was over two years away did not deter me one bit from staying on point and making my great celebration happen. Today, there is a totally different mentality about celebrating your 30th, in our family anyway. We make it a big deal. It is definitely a milestone birthday.

Around Easter of 1992, six weeks away from my 30th birthday, I started planning my big celebration. My sister Cindy and I started to talk about what we would do. I was concerned at first because my birthday, May 21, was on a Thursday that year. Then Cindy surprised me by telling me, "I am taking off from work and will be there, stay the night with you and we will make it a great time." I was thrilled that Cindy was going to make that effort. That alone was my present from her. She drove over three hours to celebrate with me.

I was very nervous to tell Tim, actually even a bit scared. There was always this fear inside of me when I had to discuss something really important when it came to me and my wants, needs or desires with Tim. I had five kids by the time I was 30, aged 12 to 3, and Tim would be the one to stay home with the kids while I went out on the town. That was something that was unusual in our life, with me being a stay-at-home mom. There was never any talk of moms needing "me time" in those days.

I was so excited to have a night with my girlfriends and my sister. I was going to celebrate me. It wasn't going to be anything extravagant, just a night out with friends, food and drinks and conversation, and yes, some music and dancing, as I love to dance. Since it was a Thursday night, there would not be many people out either. Twenty-four years ago, where I live, there were not many decent places to go for a night out with the girls.

I was a stay-at-home mom, and all my friends worked outside the home or were going to college to further their career chances. I never put myself much before anyone else. Hmmm, I really do not think I ever did that. I depended on others to put me first. I didn't make sure I was doing what I needed for myself. I didn't know I could do that.

Cindy and I were giddy, and the kids were loving the fact that Aunt Cindy was at our house, loving on her, excited to see her and be with her, and she was loving right back on them. We were all having a good time. I was already to go and looking forward to a very fun night.

Tim walked in the door from a long day at work, and saw Cindy there. He looked at me surprised and asked me what I was doing. I looked back at him stunned and said, "You know I am going out. You know Cindy took off of work to come be with me today on my 30th birthday. I told you at Easter time, over six weeks ago that I was going to be doing this."

Tim was really upset, and started huffing and puffing around, and had a pissy attitude towards me. There was no "happy birthday' to me from him. Instead, with a snarly voice he said, "Well you may as well take what I got for you, that is out on the front seat of the pickup back to the store." I had no idea what he was talking about.

I attempted to smooth things over, being kind and gentle, and we both went into another room to discuss what was going on. The peacemaker I am, I continued asking him why he was so upset and acting so rude to my sister and the kids. I knew he was going to be home with the kids, and I wanted to make sure he wasn't going to take it out on them by being grouchy with them because he did not like that I was sticking to my decision and going out.

Finally, since he did not go out to the pickup to "get what was on the front seat," I did and discovered that Tim had bought me a dozen red roses. This was completely out of character for Tim, for a few different reasons. One, he didn't like to buy flowers back then because he thought they were a waste of money, because all they do is die. Two, up to this point he had never made a big deal about my birthday. We had been married over 13 years by this time and the only other time I remember flowers from Tim was when we were dating.

I made a big deal over the roses when I brought them in from the pickup, telling him thank you and how pretty they were. I put them in a vase, kissed the kids and left with Cindy to go out and meet up with the other girls. Even though it was a quiet Thursday night out, we all still had a lot of fun. It was only us five girls and a couple of locals in the place. We laughed, we danced, we sang, we told stories, we got caught up with each other and we had a blast all night long. We even received a few rounds of free drinks.

Coming home from the evening, Cindy and I stayed up talking and giggling about how much fun we had. Tim never asked how my birthday celebration went and I never volunteered anything. With time things faded away, but we never talked about it. Nothing was ever really resolved. It was just not mentioned again.

Maybe Tim just didn't know how to deal with the fact that for a change I was not backing down. I was standing up for myself. He was not used to me keeping my word to myself, to me standing in my power. In the past I had always given in, so I did not rock the boat.

I had made up my mind though, after seeing my sister Cindy so devastated when she turned 30, I was going to celebrate myself. There was this intuitive voice within me urging me to do so. It was time for Tammy to celebrate Tammy. I showed myself that I mattered. I had lost so much of myself over the years putting everyone else first, our five children's needs always coming before mine.

Surely it wasn't my fault that Tim chose to ignore our conversation over six weeks earlier, when I told him I was going out. I was standing up for myself, but I was a bit scared deep inside, yet also there was a shift inside of me, something telling me that I deserve to have this special time, this night with me and my closest of friends. The shift said that it was ok to celebrate who I was and all I did for my family. I matter, I am worthy of doing something for myself for a change.

Watching the show *The Waltons* while growing up, I always wanted to be from a large family. I wanted the siblings and the parents and the type of relationships where they worked together and supported each other. They worked through their problems even when they were upset with each other. Every time I watched the show I would dream about this happening with me. These thoughts were ingrained within me very deep, and I forgot about them as I became a mom and wife at the age of 17. Years later, the memory came back to me of how I had always wished I was part of the Walton family. At around the age of 30, I had five children, and we were living on the Schumacher family farm (our children were the fifth generation to live on that land). It dawned on me then that I had created my own "Walton" family. Subconsciously, way before I knew what it meant to set intentions and to manifest, all those things that people talk about these days in how to create your life by choice, I had already created what deep down I had desired from a very early age in my life.

Tim and I worked on many things together; we were really good at doing that. I helped with working the farm ground, driving the swather, helping with the bales, taking care of the different birds we had, like the chickens, and helping to look after the cows. We also worked together building things, like the new house we had both decided to build, after much careful consideration on all levels. It didn't make sense to invest thousands of dollars to fix up this house that his grandparents had lived in, because it needed a new wall in the basement and other major updates.

There, was however, no deep connecting of our hearts. My dreams had faded and had been replaced with Tim's dreams. It was really his dream to create a thriving farmstead and grow that into something that maybe one day would be enough to allow us to make a living, and in the end pass down to our children.

We really needed to communicate and to share our dreams with each other, not just our meals. In my mind we needed help to do this, to learn to communicate on a level where we both heard each other, and to learn to support each other. When we had an issue, if there was a blow up, Tim wouldn't talk to me for days, and then we would just eventually go back to the way things were, and nothing ever really got worked out. Wanting everything to be ok again, I would back down. I would succumb. It is so interesting how I learned to live this life for well over a decade of my marriage. This was learned behavior that I had no idea I was doing.

I matter. I am a person. I was not just a stay-at-home mom who took care of every single thing. I was not something to be owned or controlled. This was not so much of the Love, Honor and Obey kind of thing. I was a person in a relationship and I needed to move towards being equal. I was starting to see the value in me. I was waking up to me.

What I wanted as much, possibly even more, was to know I also mattered to Tim. I didn't see then, as I see today, that Tim buying me roses for my 30th birthday was significant. In his own way he made the effort; he went out of the norm to buy me flowers. Possibly in his mind, he had made the effort, and when he came home, I was still going out. Tim stepped out of his comfort zone big time by buying me a dozen roses and when he saw Cindy's car there, he left the flowers in the pickup. It was a very awkward situation, and maybe he just didn't know how to handle it.

CHAPTER 10

The Elephant in the Room

During my early years in grade school, the church we went to as a family shut down, and we had to look around to find another church that we could all go to together. Yet nothing ever felt the same as that original church. I still remember a gathering we had in the church when I was around the age of seven. I still remember the "awe" factor about it all — going to church, gathering with all the other people, walking to the dining room to place my mom's special chocolate pudding pie with graham cracker crust on the dessert table.

Our family ended up choosing a Baptist church, which had a benefit that none of the other churches had. They had a Sunday school bus and they would come pick us up on Sunday mornings, honking the horn as they pulled up to our curb if our door wasn't open in time. When they drove us home, if we had been good and had memorized our Bible versus, we were offered the treat of sticking our hands in the glass gallon jar of gumballs to grab as many as we could before getting off the bus.

My kids were raised in a completely different faith as Tim and all his family attended a Catholic church, and I felt that I should get to know more about what my children were being taught. I grew up being told that the Catholic church was a cult, and the first time I went to a Catholic church with my best girlfriend, Brenda, at the age of 13, I remember being awestruck at how the church looked, wondering about all these windows with so many colors and all the different statues of different people. Going to mass with Brenda, I wondered why they kept kneeling, sitting, standing, kneeling again. If that wasn't enough, I was thinking, why the heck they were holding these beads on a string praying. I thought to myself, "Don't they know they can pray straight to God?" It was a completely different world I was introduced to, and I was a bit frightened and was happy when we were finally able to leave the church that day. During that experience, I never ever would have guessed that a short three years later I would be getting married in that same church, as a senior in high school who was six months pregnant.

But there was a deep part of me that really wanted to understand what my children were going to be taught. Eventually, I got involved and learned more about the beliefs, and eventually I was teaching religion classes. I crack up laughing at times thinking about this, for they did not know what they were about to unleash, asking a woman, raised as a Baptist, to come in and start teaching Catholic religion. I understood things differently, even prayed differently. When we would gather on those Friday mornings after class, and other teachers would hear me pray before our coffee time together, they would ask about it. One teacher in particular would sit in astonishment at times, and finally he got up his courage and asked me, "Tammy, where did you learn to pray like that? Tammy can you teach me to pray like that?" I was a bit stunned and looked at him and said, "You just pray like you are talking to God right here. God is right here with us. Have a conversation with God."

One of the greatest gifts I was given is Father Frank, the priest that I got to know while I was a religion teacher. I did not want to be a religion teacher, not at first. I still had two of my five children, Jenna and Tara, at home. Then, a year later, when Jenna started first grade, along came Sister Mary, who would not take "no" for an answer. She kept on at me, and I felt the pressure, especially when she said, "If you don't teach, Tammy, we may have to shut down the entire religion program." Something in me snapped and I was pissed and firmly told her, actually, I even yelled at her a bit, and said, "Don't you dare put that on me if I don't teach!" Immediately, she apologized, and in my mind I thought, "Oh shit, now I am really going to go to hell. I just yelled at a nun." I laugh about it now, and yes, I had decided by the end of that conversation to try it. I committed to teaching first grade religion classes, at least for the first semester, and ended up being there for almost four years. Sister Mary and I ended up developing a very special bond.

I also developed a special bond with Father Frank. I think at times I possibly was driving him a bit nuts as I would always be asking questions, always challenging the thoughts and beliefs of the Catholic doctrine. I wanted to understand. I was searching and he had answers. I trusted him. Once I told Father Frank, "You know Father Frank, God put me in your life for a reason." "How is that Tammy?" he said with a puzzled look on his face. "God put me in your life to keep you on your toes," I said with a grin and a chuckle in my voice.

Father Frank ended up becoming a major rock in my life. He helped me through a lot, helped me to understand so much about myself and about life in general. I was really searching for some things in my life during my 30s. He was more than a priest; he thought outside the box. You know those people in your life who you may meet for a reason, a season or a time. They are not necessarily with you for a long time, yet they mark your life, and they touch your soul so deep that their spirit will be with you forever in this lifetime. Just as the mark my grandmother made, that is what I compare it to. Father Frank was more of an influence with me than the Catholic doctrine. The bond was so strong that Tim would get frustrated with me at times, when I would come home and be talking about my time with Father Frank, and what I learned, what Father Frank said, and so on.

Tim and I continued to grow apart, never really communicating in any depth. And the underlying, cut-with-a-knife tension kept growing. We never really argued. Attempting to communicate, I would talk in normal tones, and then, after realizing I was not being heard, I would end up screaming and yelling. Then I would get pissed off that I had to resort to acting like that because at those times Tim would react like, "Oh shit, she means business."

We worked together on the new house we had agreed to build. It was a tough decision on a single income, as I still stayed at home looking after our five children. We were fortunate to have all things in place six months before the Gulf War erupted, because prices tripled but our contracts were signed with the pre-war pricing. God certainly was looking out for us. Now, our children would have their own bedrooms, their own space to grow up in. This was gift both Tim and I agreed to give them. Times were tough more often than not, and many sacrifices were made in order to afford building our new home.

We lived without furniture in the front room for over a year. The furniture in the old farm house was too old and run down, and we would rather sit on the floor or bean bag chairs than bring that old furniture into our new house.

Things like this, like building our house, Tim and I could discuss, agree on, work together on, work through, and make decisions and compromises. There was never much of an issue when it came to the bigger projects.

The frustration I was feeling over the years started to compound because I could see the good times we had, and they always gave me hope. They were the light, the flicker, that remained burning even in the darkest of times. Our marriage was not totally on the rocks. There were the family dinners, the cooking together, the gatherings we would have, enjoying together the company of others, both family and friends. There were times when it worked, and then there were those times when the tension was overwhelming and exhausting. Those tense times, when I felt I was walking on egg shells, afraid of saying or doing the wrong thing, began to wear me down. When it came to the two of us, the getting deep into our relationship, the "how do we make it work on another level," the blocks went up.

I would sit and pray to God, "How do I talk to my husband, how do I get him to hear me? God, give me the right words to say. God, you better talk to Tim, if you want this to work dammit, talk to him." I was getting to the point that I didn't really know how to reach Tim. I worked on myself. I didn't know what else to do. I had to figure out what I was doing wrong. That is what my thoughts were, *what was I doing wrong that my marriage was not as happy as I always thought it was supposed to be.* I knew that the possibility was there to make things work. Yet, I could see it slipping away and could not stop it. I no longer knew what to do. I felt myself slipping away, not just from my marriage but from my children and from myself.

With the loss of Tim's dear amazing mother, Natalie, in May 1994, I thought that now, with such a loss, maybe Tim would see how precious what we have together is — our relationship, our five kids, the house we built, all we are doing to improve the farm homestead of five generations. I thought that maybe now our relationship would mean more to him. Maybe now he would wake up to what he has. He did not. I would talk to Natalie's spirit and ask her to help me out with our marriage, to somehow reach out and talk to her son, to get through to him. I could feel our marriage failing. I could feel my grip loosening bit by bit.

If only we could have communicated in such a way that we could hear each other. Communication would have made so much of a difference. When we connect, when we communicate at the heart and soul level, that is when I know I matter to Tim. That is when I know we are on a path together.

Life is so fragile, it is so precious. Over the years, the gap between Tim and me was widening. Our relationship was gradually deteriorating and there was not much to keep it together. The glue was weakening. Our relationship was starting to slip even further from my grip.

CHAPTER 11
Slipping Away

It was a gift to me, a new lease on life, when my cousin Deb called and asked me to come to work for her part-time for three weeks a few months before Christmas. Yes, Christmas money! Ah, what a relief to be able to make some money before Christmas, helping to ease the burden of being a stay-at-home mom for 16 years. Buying Christmas presents for our entire family was going to be easier. Now that our kids were older, in junior high and high school, and very active, especially in sports, it was going to be wonderful to bring in some extra money to help out, even if it was just for three weeks.

At the age of 35, this was the first time I had worked in the corporate world. I was hired in the HR office to help do simple tasks, such as catch up on the filing and answer the phones, and with time my boss along with other department managers started to see what an asset I was. I ended up staying for more than three years.

I loved my job, yet I was not happy at home, and this was a whole new paradigm for everyone to get used to   mom now working, after I had always been at home. I was glad I had raised my kids to take care of themselves and now those teachings were showing up. The kids pulled together, yet Tim and I were pulling farther apart. This was something he was not used to. Neither one of us realized when I said yes to the job that it would end up lasting as long as it did, and that the hours would get longer.

I started to become my own person. I started to have more confidence in myself. I was more than "just a housewife and mother." There was no glory in that back in those days; it was actually looked down upon by most people, as if I wasn't really adding anything to the world. There was nothing prestigious about being a stay-at-home mom, not then, not like it is today. I had lost myself in ways I didn't realize.

Even though I was growing and coming more into my own, that still didn't help rid me of this underlying depressed feeling that continued to grow inside of me. Sure, I was even busier, having my job, volunteering at school and sponsoring different events, making sure the girls got to their games, having a blast watching them. I certainly kept busy enough so I wouldn't have to think about it, attempting to numb what was really going on inside of me. I would cry for no apparent reason, this dread inside of me growing, the darkness of not understanding what was going on inside of me. I did my absolute best to make sure it never showed up around my children. That is what we moms do, right. We hide, shove down, ignore what we are feeling in order to save our family, because the alternative is not a pretty picture. The alternative is divorce. That was not an option for me, not in my mind, not at that time in my life. I had to save my family. I had to save my marriage, somehow, some way. Yet, this overwhelming sadness was taking a hold of me and I did not understand what was going on and it was scary. I was scared because I did not know what to do. I kept going though. I kept showing up for work, which I was committed to even though I felt as if I was slipping away.

One night I came home late from work, and I had no voice. It shocked me. I was tired, I was worn out. I walked right by my children sitting with their dad at the dining room table. I remember wanting to tell them goodnight, but nothing came out of my mouth. I remember looking at them, smiling at them, yet could not say goodnight. It was still light out. Why was mom going to bed, I heard someone say.

Tim came into our bedroom, opened the door and saw me lying in bed. He started to say something, with an angry tone to his voice, then in mid sentence stopped. He saw me lying there, completely naked under the blankets, lying straight as a board with my hands on my chest as if I was in a coffin. He was asking me something. I could hear him, yet I couldn't respond. Nothing was coming out of my mouth. I could hear the words in my head, but my mouth was not moving. My eyes rolled over to look at him, acknowledging that I could hear him. The look of concern on his face grew.

I was done. Something had popped inside of me and I was done. Apparently, I was done with life. I had fought back the depression for so long that I had exhausted myself in ways I did not understand, and I was done. I couldn't move, I couldn't talk, I was a limp noodle. The stress of keeping my marriage together had broken me. I had lost my grip and was falling fast.

Tim told me later that looking down at me as I lay in bed, the pain he saw in my eyes reminded him of the pain he saw in his mom's eyes two days before she died. There was something in me that was telling me that if I went to sleep I was not going to wake up the next morning. I felt as if my soul was starting to leave my body. I was broken and I was dying in more ways than one. I wonder now, as I am sharing this, is this the pain of a "lost soul," the pain of the "unspoken woman." Many years later, I was told by a doctor that I had been suffering from broken heart syndrome, which he was in the process of helping me to heal and become whole again.

Tim was so frightened that he called Father Frank. He didn't know what to do, but he knew he needed to do something. He got me out of bed. He had to dress me as I had no strength to dress myself. He helped me walk to the van. He drove. I don't remember the kids, where they were, what they were thinking. It was a bit of a blur to me, and still is to a point, over 15 years later.

As we pulled into the driveway to park in front of the friary, where Father Frank lived, he was standing in the doorway. I remember thinking how odd that was, thinking why was he waiting for us at the front door, ready to usher me, us, into his office. As he walked down the steps to greet Tim and me, I saw fear in Father Frank's eyes as he looked into my eyes. I saw the fear of not knowing what to do or how to help. I realize now that his eyes were a reflection of mine. It was the fear I had in my own eyes, the fear of not knowing what to do for I was done and leaving this earth and all the pain behind. It was if it was not my choice anymore. It was more that it was my soul.

Father Frank sat Tim and me down across from each other. Father Frank sat on my left side, and I remember his first question. He was attempting to keep his composure as I could hear uncertainty in his voice as he asked, "What is going on?"

Both Tim and Father Frank looked at me, and with every ounce of energy I had left, out of my mouth came in a very low whisper, "I'm done, I am done, I'm done and do not know what to do and I do not trust him to pull us through this," as I pointed to

Tim. My voice started to come back as we sat there and discussed things, the three of us. Eventually I was feeling more life inside of me. Was it because I was finally speaking my truth? I was finally telling how I felt at the deepest level, and yes, somebody was listening. They both were listening. Tim was listening, and I think actually hearing me.

Knowing that our issues were beyond his expertise, Father Frank recommended that Tim and I go see Father Bill, who specializes in the area that we required. The next day we called and made the first appointment. For the next few months, things improved remarkably. Things get better when you do the work. We would meet with Father Bill one-on-one and as a couple, learning new ways to communicate, new ways to be with each other. We were talking to each other, with each other, in ways I don't remember doing before, connecting on new levels that we were discovering. I was feeling loved by Tim, and my heart was starting to open once again. It was refreshing, and the hope of it all working out was growing. Yes, it was working out, we were doing the work.

I never understood what happened one day a few months after we started the counseling. I was sitting at the dining room table, working on paperwork, preparing our taxes, you know that time of year, getting ready to go to our accountant. Tim was in the kitchen drying dishes for me, something that was totally out of character, because that was the "woman's job." It was filling my heart so full of love. He was helping me out, and I felt loved and taken care of. Yeah, I know it may sound a bit funny that a simple act of helping me with the dishes can mean so much to me, but it still does to this day. It fills my love bucket.

I could feel the gleam of love coming out of my eyes, as I looked up and saw him in the kitchen, thinking to myself, *this is working out, wow, this is really working out!* I was so full of joy, and I could feel my heart and my soul opening more, and this new level of love coming forth. This was a true miracle for me.

Then, in a blink of an eye, it all changed. Tim looked at me while he was drying that one dish, walked across the kitchen to the counter by the stove, and with an angry voice yelled at me, "I'm done." He threw down the towel, saying, "I'm done. I'm done. You do your thing and I will do my thing. I'm done!" Then he walked out of the north door of the house, and went to do his work around the farm.

Sitting at the table, my jaw dropped, and my mind raced, thinking, "What the hell just happened?" Did I just dream what I saw and heard? How could things turn so quickly? Of course, my mind went to the old way I used to think. "What did I do? What did I say? What did I not say?" For the life of me I had no clue. Nothing warned me that was going to fly out of Tim's mouth. Once again, I was devastated.

Even though Tim chose to quit the counseling sessions, I continued on. I had to for my own sanity. I was not going back to where I was. I was only moving forward. When you put in the work, relationships work, life works. Things get better. Life starts to expand and new levels appear. Keep doing the work. No matter, what keep doing the work. No matter how tired you feel, even when you don't think it is doing any good, keep doing the work. It does pay off. In the long run, it always pays off. When you do the work, you will live with no regrets.

I kept going to Father Bill. Something inside of me compelled to keep moving forward with his help. I promised myself I would never ever get to a point in my life again where I felt my soul was leaving my body. I would do all I could to make sure I would never go down that road of depression again. I felt that continuing to go to Father Bill was one way to make sure that never happened. I knew I still needed help, and more than ever now to assist me in dealing with my husband, who was no longer willing to do the work.

Father Bill told me in one of our sessions, giving me permission to get a divorce, "Tammy, one person cannot make a relationship." What we had was not working. Yet that was not an option for me. I was not ready to do the divorce thing. Instead, I found a different way to cope, and this time it was about growing me, finding me, becoming more of me and bringing forth what I am here to do. I started diving into personal growth and personal development. I started to find the right teachers, mentors and programs. When it comes down to it, we are responsible for ourselves. We are the ones accountable for how our lives are, for how we are living, for our own happiness. I was starting to learn that, and even though I didn't like what I was hearing and learning all the time, I knew this to be true. I was taking my life into my own hands, and I was learning to no longer be dependent on another person for my own happiness.

The gift of me was really what the troubles in my marriage gave me. I am the optimistic one. I am always looking for the silver lining in any situation. I truly believe I would not be who I am today, and have the ability to help all the people I do — my clients, friends, coworkers, family — had I not experienced the difficult things in my marriage and in my life. Those things made me dig deep inside of myself to grow me. I was realizing that I do matter and I was beginning to take hold and started to solidify myself.

I learned that I am worthy, and I know that you are worthy also, no matter what situation you are in, have been in, no matter where you are at in life, what you have thought, said or did, that you may have some regrets about. You are worthy and you do matter.

Our marriage plodded along. The day-to-day things held our attention and kept us connected to some degree. Tim was working out of town eight months out of the year and that helped, as we did not have to be around each other constantly. And when he was in town during the winter months I would be traveling, working on my business, going to workshops, doing my own thing just as he was doing his own thing. Staying busy growing me was another escape mechanism to help me not really deal with the elephant in the room, and I was good with that for the time being. For over a decade we remained together, living as roommates for the most part.

CHAPTER 12

Turning the Corner

I committed to myself that would never let anyone ever take me down to that dark place again. I was broken wide open. I was completely raw and had to work on putting myself back together.

I remember the thought, "Tammy, watch what you ask for," because before this darkest times, I would always ask God, "Why can't I feel my children's love?" I knew they loved me, and I could feel my love for them, yet I could not for the life of me *feel* their love for me. I used to ask this question over and over. Over the years, as I started to heal myself from the broken shell I was, a profound new awareness started to take place. I started to feel, really feel, the love, not only from my children, which was big, but also an intense depth of love that was beyond anything I could have ever imagined. To this day it continues to grow and expand in ways that are beyond me at times. I know that I know it. This love poured upon me and was brought up within me through all those years of healing. That Divine Love is what I now am able to give to others, and most importantly myself, as I love to love. I think this way: in order to be the love that I am today, I had to break, to get to that point and be rebuilt from a cellular level, from the inside out.

In the fall of 2002, I felt a bit of slipping off track, and I knew I had to get a hold of me before it went too far. Remember I had promised myself that I would never ever allow myself to go back to the point of the empty shell, the dark and lost period of my life. As I was standing in my bedroom looking out over the fields, I started to cry. I fell to my knees in despair and prayed out loud with a demanding urgency, "God, help me, and if it is to be men I am to learn from, let them be men that I can honor, respect, love and admire. Let it be men that I can trust and that I can learn from, and at the top." I was demanding this from God. I was tired of messing around.

For years and years, I had always felt there was something bigger I was supposed to do. I came here with a mission. I was at a loss, however, and everything I tried it seemed to never be the right thing. In some ways I felt lost and alone and not able to explain this burning desire to learn the unknown purpose within me. As I sought help to understand, I would hear things like, "Tammy, you have five kids. That is a great purpose. Maybe that is it." But being the great mom that I was, the depth of unconditional love I felt for my children, being there for them as much as I was, committed to them, and more, still did not take away that fire within my belly. I always knew there was more I was to do. Yet, no one ever really understood that part of me.

I wanted to meet Robert and Mark in person at an event they were holding in regards to their book. I do not know why, but there was this push within me telling me that I had to be there, to somehow make sure I was there. Tim never really said anything. He pretty much shrugged and had an attitude of, *whatever*.

At that point in my life, April 2003, at the age of 40, I really didn't travel too much out of state, not to something big like this, a conference where there would be hundreds of other people. I felt that my youngest child, Tara, only 13, still needed her mom to be around all the time. That was my frame of mind. It took a lot of courage for me to go. This was the first time I left my children for an extended period of time, almost a week, to do something for me.

Thank goodness Debbie was going with me, as I could not imagine going alone. That was a really big deal for two Kansas girls to just pick up and say they were going to Orlando for a week. You just didn't do things like that back in those days. I was determined to be there and to walk through any obstacle, any fear that would come up.

While sitting in the audience, on the left side of the stage and two rows back, I was mesmerized by Robert and Mark. They were so funny. I was cracking up laughing, so much that I snorted. My laugh caused Robert to stop in his tracks right there on stage. He shook his head a bit and asked, "Who is that woman with that laugh out there?"

"Oh shit, he is talking about me!" I was scared of getting kicked out since I broke his concentration. I had interrupted his presentation. I attempted to shrink down in my seat, oblivious to the fact that Debbie was pointing to me.

Robert looked right at me from the stage, and in front of over 500 people said to me, "I love your laugh. I want to pay you for your laugh" Robert handed me a $20 bill right there in front of everyone, from the stage. My mind was spinning and my body was sweating.

As I waited in line later that same day, to get both Robert's and Mark's autographs in my book, I had people coming up to me asking, "Do you have a card with your laugh on it?" The thought in my head was, "You can do that? Huh? Really."

Finally I was standing in front of Robert with my book in hand, and before I could say anything, out of his mouth came, "Tammy, I love your laugh, and do you know, I have met millions of people in my lifetime, and no one, not anyone, has a laugh like yours. Your laugh is unique and different, and that is how you know that your laugh is not just a gift. Your laugh is a spiritual gift."

For those precious moments as he looked deep into my eyes, and I into his, we were the only two that existed in that room. I knew on some level it was more than Robert talking to me. His soul was reaching my soul with this profound new realization about myself. Sometimes experiences have no words that can come close to explaining the depth and awe of what took place. This was one of those times. I knew God was speaking to me through Robert Allen in that moment.

I felt in a bit of a daze for the rest of the four days or so while at the event. I had so many people come up to me to tell me how much they loved my laugh, to give me helpful hints on what to do and what to create. I started to see that there was more to me, more than being "just a mom." There was more of Tammy here and I was enjoying immensely being on this particular path of discovery.

"I have a gift, I really have a gift" was one of the thoughts that was going through me. I have been searching and asking what was so special about me most of my life, and now at the age of 40 I was being shown that something I had all my life, something that was natural and always a part of who I was, was a gift. And not just a gift, a spiritual gift. It had always been there in the palm of my hand.

I realized I had something that was real, and it was such a part of me. I had no idea it was a gift because for most of my life I was ridiculed for my laugh. I was told to be quiet, to shush, and people would give me the oddest of looks. They would get up and walk away from me and go sit somewhere else. I was accused of being fake in order to draw attention to myself. Not only is my laugh contagious, it can get really outrageous and loud and then I begin to snort. It's pretty funny I think, yet some people have shunned me because of it. So, why in the world would I ever think of my laugh as a gift?

That all changed in April 2003 and I am ever so grateful it did. On a deeper level, I was given permission that day. I was given permission to be me, to be all me. My dear friends opened up something inside of me. It was a spring of life that started to come forth. I was ok, I can be, do and have all. In a moment I saw that, and more importantly I felt that. Over the years to come I would recognize that more and more, and work hard on rediscovering who I was and shed the layers of discontent from me.

I knew I was supposed to record my laugh. How in the world does someone do that? I was now entering a whole new world. I was shy when it came to me and putting myself out there, especially in such a new and unique way as to record my laugh. When Debbie and I returned from Orlando, she was the one who found someone to record me. If not for Debbie, I am not sure to this day if I would have ever stepped into this part of who I am.

Yet, I was still scared. I was putting it off, making excuses, catching up in the house after being gone for a week, and Debbie and I were scheduled to go to a free workshop in Denver three weeks after returning from Orlando, so I didn't make it happen.

In Denver, still in April 2003, we were sitting at a real estate seminar, and again, the speaker was funny. I was laughing, and this being such a short time after Orlando, I was still not realizing on a deeper level the significance of my laugh and how it helps others. During a break a gentleman came up to the table where we were sitting and said, "Who is that lady with that laugh over here?" He seemed to have a bit of a snarl to his voice, and I thought he was upset. Intimidated by him, I quietly responded, "Um, that was me. Why? Did I make you mad?" He looked at me wide eyed and said, "No, I love your laugh!"

I was stunned, here again was another sign, another person telling me, "I love your laugh." It was becoming more and more real to me, these people telling me this. It was as if this was the first time in my life I was able to hear, really hear, the compliments about my laugh. I immediately turned to Deb and said, "Debbie, I need your help, and you have to keep me accountable. I have to record my laugh. I have to. God is talking to me through these people. I just know it." God, the Universe, Source, Higher Self, whatever you chose to call that Higher Power. I believe we do get messages in all types of ways.

Within days of returning from Denver, I called the recording studio, the phone shaking in my hand, tears streaming down my cheeks, fear grasping me and holding me tight, attempting to take me out, and I made the appointment to start the process of recording my laugh. By birthday, May 21, 2003, I had my first CD completed. Wow. I had not just recorded my laugh but also a bunch of funny stories about my life, so it really was more than I ever thought possible.

Yeah, I had my CDs in hand. I was taking them to California. I was going to another personal development course. I was committed. I was in a major transition in my life. Now, my life was leaning towards me and the changes I wanted. Actually, it was more than that. I had to, I was required to, shift and make changes in my life, in me, internally. I had committed to myself that I would never be taken back into those dark days. Everything I was getting introduced to I was resonating with. There was this internal fire within me. I was hungry, hungry to learn, to grow, to discover who I was and what this new world I stepped into was about. The burn inside of me was so big no one could stop me. I couldn't stop myself, and I did not want to.

Some people may say I went overboard on person development, yet this is what was saving my life. I was finding me. For the first time in my life I was finding me, and I had no idea how lost I had been. I do not fit in a box. I have tried that. I have tried to be what others wanted me to be, and each and every time I would get depressed. I was obliterating the box. Now I say, "Box, what box? There is no box for Tammy," and I giggle.

All the work I was doing on myself was helping me to make the decisions from that point forward that impacted me, to bring value back to my life, back to my dreams. I was learning to no longer allow things to be brushed under the rug. I was sweeping things out that were under the rug in many areas of my life.

The light went on inside of me! Hell, I really matter, really *matter*. At one particular small workshop, something popped, and I realized that the power within me was unlimited. I had unlimited potential if I chose to use it. I had a new dedication to life. I was learning and really getting how powerful I truly am. I started teaching other women the same thing, never wanting anyone to suffer in the silence as I did.

We all have this potential, no matter what age in life we start to discover it. We all have it in our own ways, yet it is up to each one of us individually to act upon it. You have it within you to develop our own potential, and I believe you can. I know you can, if you choose. Hear me, if you choose. That is one of the first steps: we each have to choose.

I had a new dedication to life, to my life. I was now creating my life by design, not by default, step-by-step as I was learning how to do so. It was not always easy, yet I was determined. The people that I was being introduced to were giving me the tools.

Let me share this with you. Some of these steps were painful, yet they were absolutely necessary. It was not always easy, and sometimes it was lonely, because as I grew, others were being left behind and that was scary at times. That made me even more grateful for the new friendships I was making, the new group of people I was being introduced to. That in part is what helped me to keep going

I was being shown the tools. It was up to me to decide on which ones were a fit for me, and then to actually use them. Get up and do it. You have the power and potential to do it. That is what makes life worthwhile. Get up off the couch and use the tools. And get out of your own way.

Making the choice to get up and do the work, that is what makes relationships work, that is what makes your career work, that is what make your business work, that is what makes your parenting work, that is what makes life worthwhile. Make the choice to get up and do it.

When you actually get up and do it, that is what I found in the second start. I have a different approach to life. I am making a shift happen. I am going out and doing the things that make my life better. This comes about only because I have chosen to do these things, the things that I am greatly benefiting from that are bringing more of me back to me.

When I work with my clients one-on-one, or in a group, we start to rediscover their gifts. I remind them to recall, to ask themselves, "What is natural for you, what has always come so natural, without thinking?" That is usually a gift, your gift. Sometimes it is something so simple, like my laugh, and that is only one of the many gifts I have discovered in the last 14 years. What is it for you? What comes natural? What have you had compliments about?

Once we discover our gifts, it is time to decide to use them. It is time to bring them forth no matter what! No matter how scared we are. If we desire our soul to grow and become all we came here to be and to make the impact I know each and every one has the power to do, we have to commit to using our gifts and allowing our soul to shine through us.

I was getting my life back and was following my dreams. I was seeing glimpses of my potential. I took Jenna, our second youngest, to California with me, introducing her to this new way of thinking, desiring to expose her to something new and different before she started her senior year. I was starting to take my dreams seriously. I was making decisions to develop my life. I was determined to give Jenna this gift of this trip, and while there we met people that opened up the possibility to go sailing, to stay on sailboat overnight, seeing dolphins playing in the ocean.

This doesn't happen by luck or happenstance. I was now making conscious decisions about what I desired in my life. Step-by-step, this has been a process, an unfolding, especially over the last 15 years. The unfolding will continue all of my life as it will yours, which means we are growing. As long as you are growing, you are alive. Once we quit growing, we start to die.

I am choosing life! What are you choosing? I am here to help you if you choose life! You have the potential, yet you have to act on it. Sometimes, you have to get up at 3:00 a.m. to make it happen, like I did to write the pages of the book. Taking action is what is required of us. Once we make the decision, whatever that is for us, and we must put action to those decisions. That is when more potential, more magic, more of us gets revealed and comes forth.

Being around like-minded people is a must in life. We all need to associate with people who help us see what we desire to be and do and have in our life. People who see our greatness and help us to bring it out and help us embrace it and develop it. Reach out to me at www.transformintojoy.com and see if working together is the right thing to help you get to your next level in life. To help you create your Heaven on Earth. It is not just a choice. It is an absolute must! Keep growing!

CHAPTER 13

No Elephants

I was so tired of hearing that I had to deal with the elephant in the room. What damn elephant? I was not getting what the hell was meant by that. There is no elephant; call it what it s. Here is the difficult issue. We have to deal with it, so we can move on. Quit skirting around what is at hand, and say exactly what you see so I can get to it, do the hard work, move through it, and be better in spite of it. I was ready to face the difficult issues, talk about the unmentionables, figure out what to do next, but I needed some help.

I was so tired of the bullshit of people, even mentors, being vague about what they saw was going on in me, around me, and not coming out to just say what the hell they really meant. For years, I would hear, "Tammy, you gotta take care of the Elephant in the room." I got to the point after hearing this term used so much by different people, some of them mentors, that I would get pissed off, asking what was meant by saying that. Wanting someone to tell me, help me to see through their eyes what the damn elephant was they were talking about, and what did they really mean? Show me, walk me with me through it, be with me through these tough moments. That was tough to do on my own; apparently I was a bit blind.

I needed the straight up facts. I desired that type of coaching, that mentoring of "Let's get to it, deal with it, work on it, and get through it to keep moving with clarity," That is why I am so committed to working like this with my own clients in my coaching business, because I never want someone to feel alone to figure out and go through the tough unmentionables, as I felt I was so many times. Tell it like it is with a base of profound love. That is how I am, because that is how I wanted others to be with me. Life is way too precious to waste on beating around the bush and not getting to the point as quickly as possible. My clients absolutely love this aspect about me and for that reason have profound breakthroughs in the process.

Although I had been on the road of self improvement, of finding and developing my self worth, I was still unsure of this whole idea of deprogramming and reprogramming myself. I didn't understand this when people were talking about it. That was not so long ago, only a few years. I finally figured this out as a blink of an eye just a bit ago in 2013.

Tell me what to do, then I can do it. When I am down, the last thing I need is a word puzzle. Just tell me like it is, dammit, if you are a person who can see into my life, yet I am so close to that I do not see. This was extremely frustrating, especially for someone like me who wants to always know how I can be better. Life is too precious to be messing around with tough issues and not getting to the core of the issues and dealing with them. Yes, I know how tough this can be. That is why I am determined to help people as much as I can, and as many people as I can. I have been there. I know the pain and the value of walking through the fear and out to the other side. I know how important it is to have certain people by your side as you walk through these times in your life. I know some people do not want to look at their problems, yet that is not me. You've got issues and you gotta deal with them.

Tell me and show me by example. We are into some hard work here. I am willing to do the hard work, and sometimes I require to be led in the right direction to do so.

The issue was my marriage, not an elephant in the room. I so appreciate my friends who have no filters. We love unconditionally, and there is no pussy-footing around, especially when it comes to our lives and telling it how we see it. My friend Michelle is no exception to this, and that is why I love her so, even though sometimes it is years in between talking. I met Michelle in September 2003, at Enlightened Warrior Camp, held in Canada that year. We developed a bond that would last a lifetime after all we experienced together during those five days on deeply intense immersion into our greatest strengths, our astounding capabilities and seeing what our powerful selves and our remarkable lives could be really be.

It had been years since Michelle and I had last spoken, yet when we connected again on the phone at the beginning of 2013, it was as if we had never been apart. As we were catching up on our lives and I was telling her about life with Tim, she stopped me, in mid conversation and said to me, "Tammy that is the same old story you have told me ever since I met you over 10 years ago. You either need to shut up about it or do something about it. You know I love you girl, but enough is enough already." Yikes, I was still talking about my marriage, how unhappy I was, how nothing had changed in all these years. *What the world was going on with me,* I thought to myself. I either need to shut up or do something about it. My marriage was killing me, killing my spirit.

Her tough love in that moment shook me. I seriously felt she was reaching through the phone and grabbing me by the shoulders, shaking me, telling me to wake up. It was a conversation that made me stop in my tracks and take a long hard look at my marriage, at this relationship, one of the most important in my life and how it was determining my life. That conversation shook me up enough to know, to see, that it was time, no more excuses Tammy. It was time to do what I had to do to leave my marriage. I had been putting it off, too terrified to take the steps that were required to make "shift" happen.

I love Michelle so much. I know it took tremendous courage to say what she was compelled to say. I know it came from the base of love and trust that our friendship was built upon. She desired the best for me and saw where I was coming up short in my life.

I know how hard it is, how scary it is to tell a friend the truth, especially about the tough subjects, not knowing how that person will react. You put it all on the line, trusting in that friendship, that it will get you through the tough deep subjects and the calling of each other out on our stuff. I know those questions that go through our mind, "Will she be mad at me? Will she talk to me again? Will I hurt her feelings? I am so scared of what she will think if I really tell her the truth." This is where the trust of that relationship comes in. For if we are not able to trust in our relationships, to tell the truth, then really is it a relationship worth keeping? If we cannot speak the truth without fear, then what are we doing in that relationship to begin with, what is going to happen to our relationship? We need to look at our relationships where we are too afraid to say the truth. Is it that person or is it ourselves? Those tough subjects that we need to bring up every now and then may not be their truth, yet once we bring it up to them, we can discuss it with them. Yes, things can sting, and we can work together through the sting. If the relationship falls apart, because of you bringing something up, then it was never meant to be for a lifetime. It was only there for a season and maybe only for that reason.

Things were changing in my life. More things had to change. Life is about changes. One of my personal mantras now, especially when I get a bit scared, is "Embrace the Change". I had to deal with the issue of my marriage, now that I could see that it was what so many others kept referring to the elephant in the room. The rest of the things under the rug had to be pulled out, looked at, dealt with, so I knew exactly where I stood and where to go from there.

Honestly, at times I still get really pissed off, even now, as I am sharing this. Knowing so much time was wasted, time I cannot get back, time that is precious because it took so long to figure out the whole time people were actually talking about my marriage. It was not some damned elephant in the room, it was my marriage. We waste too much time achieving nothing when we do not know where we are going, or how we are going to get there.

It is not fun, but the rewards are worth it. It made me grow, it made me strong. Walking out of my marriage was the most terrifying thing I ever did in my life. I had no idea what I was doing. I was going into completely uncharted waters. I was throwing myself out into the cold world. I was on my own for the first time at the age of 52. And I did not even know really who were going to be my friends when I walked out on my husband, walked out on my marriage. At the age of 17, I went from my father's house to husband's house. I had never lived on my own, never known that was even an option. How could I think that was an option with raising five children? How would I, a stay-at-home mom for the first 16 years of my married life, know the first thing about being able to do such a thing? When I did start working outside the house, I made some money, but never enough to raise 5 children, thinking I had to be the only one to do that.

I put everything on the line. I risked everything. I risked losing my entire family. I risked losing my identity and everything else that defined me. I was known as Tammy with five kids. I had 10 grandchildren. I risked being severely judged, people thinking I was crazy. What was I doing at the age of 52 leaving my marriage, "Oh but Tammy you have it all," I would hear people say. "You have the family and the marriage and all that others wished so much that they had." I was terrified, knowing that my leaving was about to shake up everything my children had grown up and known and felt secure in for over 34 years. I had no idea, didn't really think about the devastating effects on my grandchildren. Yet, I still knew, I had to do this for me. All I knew I would have is my laugh, yet the situation took that too, to the deepest levels. I have never been this far before in this area of my life. I didn't know what things would be crushed from me, taken from me.

Asking myself, "Who is Tammy without a man in her life?" That was a new revelation for me at the age of 52, something I had never experienced before. Thinking about leaving is one thing. I had been doing that for years, off and on. Actually taking steps into this new area was something completely foreign to me.

I had no idea what I was doing. I didn't know how to start, as odd as that may sound. How do I start the process of leaving my marriage? It is not as simple as packing up and going back home. I had no home to go to, no mother, no father to help me out, let alone guide me. It took someone else to help me settle my nerves, my anxiety and suggest to me to go see a lawyer and see what my options were. "Oh, well that is a good idea." I had never thought of that though.

Pulling back the curtains on the unknown and stepping into this new area of my life, as frightening as it was, in time gave me a new sense of confidence. It helped me to come into a higher level of dependability upon myself, trusting myself, knowing I was safe with me, that somehow, some way, I knew that I knew I was going to make it through. There was a new level of determination rising up in me.

I never thought my decision to leave was going to be the best gift I ever gave to my family and my marriage. My kids now had a dad they had not known at this level. Walls would come down, paradigms would shift and be no more, because this broke Tim, and they all pulled together to help their dad make it through. They saw a new part of their dad come to life, hugging them more than ever, saying "I love you" at every opportunity, having conversations that opened them all up to a new understanding of each other.

With all the hurt that was going on with everyone affected by this, including myself, even with all of that, I was experiencing a new level of happiness I never knew existed. I was no longer walking on egg shells. I had made a decision and I followed through with it, as damned tough as it was. This huge weight that I had carried for so many years, oblivious to it, was being lifted. I was learning so much about myself in the process, learning to love myself on different levels, to be with myself, working through the confusion of being happy, of new revelations of awareness, yet still having those breakdown moments of gut-wrenching sadness as I was working through the entire process step by step.

One step at a time is how we get through the tough issues. You need to make a decision, one way or another. Do it, you could talk about it forever, but you need to do it. There is a power in making a decision and staying committed to that decision. It is time to take off the sugar-coating, addressing the problem that is the problem. Talk about it, write about it. Let's admit it, there are serious issues in our lives, and we need to quit making light of them so we can make a difference in who we are and how we are living in our lives and how we allowed our hopes and dreams to slip away, how we allowed our boundaries to be compromised by putting up with, instead of standing strong in spite of.

Instead of listening to others who say, "You can't go back," in fact you must go back. You have to deal with those things from the beginning. I understand the pain that is caused by doing that. I did that with my mother when I was in my early 20s. I lost my family when I was 13, with the divorce of my parents, and I felt abandoned and left alone to figure it all out. I wanted to talk to my mom about the divorce, and she would have no part of it. She said, "It's over, it's done, it's swept under the rug now and you cannot go back." Yet there was still a hole in my heart from that loss. Over a decade later, in my early 40s, I approached the subject again. This time, however, I prefaced it by saying, "Mom, I need to talk to you about the divorce, not to blame you, more importantly to have you hear me." My mom was then open. As soon as I shared what was on my mind and in my heart and I knew my mom had heard me and acknowledged my feelings, again not blaming anyone, sharing from where I was, instantly that hole in my heart healed. That was the result of my 13 year old girl being able to share her feelings 30 years later. And just as important, I was retrieving a part of me that was lost for all those decades. I literally felt and saw pieces of me coming back to me.

This is what I call Soul Retrieval and part of what I help my clients with. A magical essence happens when you do this work. The result is so much worth the difficulty of going through this. It can be really tough. I am not making light of this. As difficult it may seem, since this is not the fun part of life, it is worth it 100 times over. You have to deal with it and the result will be well worth it. This is hard work that yields results.

I encourage you to sit in silence with yourself, or with a valued friend, and make a list. Think about what happened earlier in your life that was swept under the rug, ignored, made light of. Those are usually the things which are causing the major issues currently in life, years later. I understand this can be tough, yet we must do this work in order to clear it up, transform it, heal from it and live a life that is more full, complete and joyful. I help my coaching clients to do this, and more and the end results are outstanding.

Depending where you are at in life, you may desire to start with the small things and work up to the bigger ones, in order to not go into a state of overwhelm. Do not do this alone. In my opinion and experience, having someone by your side through these processes is vital. The problem may not be your marriage; it can be something from childhood, an issue with a parent, sibling or friend, a past relationship that you are still suffering from for some reason, or an incident that happened at some time in your life, such as in school. One step at a time, I know you can do it. Some things may go by the wayside, because when one issue is really looked at and addressed, other things that have bothered you may no longer have the charge around them anymore. Acknowledging that something "stung," no matter what it was, is a major step into healing that. Your starting place could be a casual remark that might not have been intended to hurt. Acknowledgement is a major step forward. You can do this! I believe in you!

CHAPTER 14

Leaving

I woke up on Sunday, November 10, 2013, to face this major event in my life.

"Keep it together Tammy, keep it together," I would remind myself throughout the day. My stomach still churns and tears glisten in my eyes as I write this three years later, as if it was yesterday. I was 51 and I had never lived on my own. I was now going to be the sole person to rely on. It was not only the physical aspect of setting up a household on my own; it was also the emotional side of living alone for the first time in my life, after half a century of being with others. Now my life was going to be totally my responsibility. I was about to embark on self-reliance. So many things were adding up to be overwhelming, hence the need for my reminders to myself to "keep it together."

I picked a day that had no special significance, like a birthday, for me or my family. However, it was hard picking the right day and the right time. "When the hell really would be the right time?" It was very hard to make that decision, knowing I was about to tear my family apart, knowing I was going to hurt them. What are my kids going to say? How are they going to react? Will they hate me to the point of never speaking to me again? Will they still love me at all? These questions and others would intensify as the day to leave got closer. There is never a "right time" for what I was about to do, for what after years of thinking about it, I was finally going to do it. But I had to do this for me, I had to leave to save me.

The emotional aspects were 10 times heavier on my chest than that actual physical part of leaving. In retrospect, I realize it was the closest thing to a death, not only for my children, also my grandchildren. I never once thought about how this all would affect my grandchildren, but it did.

I do not like to admit that I was sneaky, but that is what I felt I had to be. With the dynamics of my marriage at that point, I felt that being sneaky was my only option. I totally admit it. I was looking out for me and I had to do what it took to protect me in every way possible and to allow me to stay strong and make sure I did not back down this time. I would sneak around, going to look at apartments, finding my apartment, doing this all on my own. I moved my clothes out, and few other things, things that would not be missed, one small car load at a time.

The last Sunday family gathering for me was the day. Everyone was coming to the farm for family dinner, and this was the last family dinner I would be making, I prepared it with so much love, more than ever before, so aware that I wanted this memory to be with me forever. I don't know if I had ever been so aware of all the small details of every little thing I was doing. I was paying attention to everything, taking it all in, not knowing if I would ever be welcomed back into this house.

I was compounding the emotions I already had in me with the guilt of how I was handling my moving out. When my daughter Crystal went to put the laundry away in my drawers, she saw them empty and asked me what was going on. I really now regret that I told her the truth. I was so tired of being out of integrity.

Yet, I think I should have lied that one more time. I could have said I was getting new furniture. Instead, I told her the truth, in the middle of that day, and I put this unbearable burden on her. Dammit, I wish I could take that one back. For this I am truly sorry Crystal, and I hope one day you can forgive me for putting such an unbearable burden on you. She went through the rest of day knowing and attempting to hide it. I kept checking on her, looking out the window to see how she was doing as she was putting up Christmas decorations, seeing her cry uncontrollably at times. I should have known better. I was the mom in this situation. Damn, what did I just do to my child, putting that heavy load on her? I continue to have tears about this one, hoping one day she can forgive me for putting so much on her at that time. It is incredible how thinking straight and being on top of it just does not happen when going through such a traumatic event. This is why you need a support team around you, and with you.

Tim had fallen asleep on the floor while the kids were still there. One by one they were leaving, the last of them at about 10:00 p.m. I stood there looking at Tim, seeing him sleep, knowing I was going to have to wake him up. I could have just walked out without telling him. That would have been the easy way. I was praying so hard, asking God to help through this. "Come on God I really need your help on this one."

While I was pacing back and forth, telling myself to stay strong, not to chicken out, Tim woke up on his own. At my request we sat at the bar in the kitchen and I told him. I told him that I was leaving. I had my own apartment. I told him that I was done. Tim begged me to stay, saying we can work this out. I told him we had been down that road before too many times. It was the hardest thing I have ever done in my life, actually following through my commitment to myself and walking out the door as he was completely torn up and crying and begging me not to leave. I walked out and I felt like I was going to throw up.

I arrived at my apartment, stomach churning, tears dropping from my cheeks. Even though I was in a bit of a daze, I felt a sense of relief. I felt the load starting to lift from my chest. I did it. I did not chicken out. I stood up for myself, as hard as it was, and I did what I knew I had to do for me. I took the first major step in saving my life. It was ok for me to go from a 3600 square foot house to an 800 square foot apartment. I was going to be ok, I reassured myself, lying on my air mattress as I drifted off to sleep.

I had taken the first step, recognizing that I am a person. It was not so much about getting my own apartment. It was taking the step towards recognizing that I am a human being and that I do have value and recognizing that I deserved better than what I was allowing in my life.

My emotions were all over the place, and I fought through it, knowing this was for me. For a few days I would be doing very well, and then something would shake the ground of confidence and I would be in a bad way for a while. But a sense of relief was washing over me, and I knew I would be ok. Wow, I did it. I had enough courage to do what I required to do for me. My confidence in me was growing day by day. I knew I did the right thing for me. I knew I had enough courage to get on with building the rest of my life.

Girl, you have to have a support system. Somehow I knew that. Never make yourself an island. You have got to reach out and ask for help. Do not think for one moment you can go through something so critical as leaving a relationship, especially one of 30 plus years, alone. I had close friends who helped me through this time in my life. They saw how I was dwindling. I had the type of friends who would ask about both me and Tim. They cared about us both and wanted the best for us both. That is the type of support I needed. "Tammy, what can I do to help you?" "Tammy, how is Tim doing?" That is what I needed from my real friends at that time!

Build your support network with close friends, with people who value you and even if they do not understand the pain you are going through. People who see your pain. Support does not mean that they just talk nice to you. You need people who will tell you straight. This is not the time to have people in your life that want to wallow in your misery, who say, "Oh poor Tammy." No, we need the strong people. You gotta get the support of people who you trust, who love you and who will tell you straight out what they think.

Even though this was a time of mourning, since this is a death in its own right, make sure you do not go down the stream of self pity and wallowing in sadness. There is a fine balance. There is also a time to pull on the big girl panties and start moving forward. That is when you require those strong loving friends to pull you up and walk beside you through this. No self pity allowed. Those type of friends you can rely on. And it is ok to have both male and female friends.

Valuable things are never easy. Even though this was the toughest thing in my life to do, it needed to be done. Having five children naturally was a piece of cake compared to making this decision, to walking through this most critical event in my life.

Quit being so damned politically correct and soft. When it is shitty, tell me it is shitty, and tell me how to fix it. I did not come to you for "poor me" soft and gentle, hug-wuggy stuff.

If you fix the big things, the little things will take care of themselves. When the big things are going right, it does not matter if the lid is off the peanut butter or the toothpaste is squeezed in the middle. If things are going good, the little things can be adjusted along the way. Leaving off the lid is not the issue; it is the bigger thing. The little things are non issue when the big things are ok.

CHAPTER 15
The Papers Arrive

In mid April 2014, on a Friday after 5:00p.m., five months after I had moved out of our home, I was working late in town my executive sales job for a communications company. Thank goodness everyone else was gone for the day because what I least expected was about to happen. Tim phoned, saying "I am coming over, I have something".

Tim pulls up and while sitting in his work pickup, tosses the divorce papers at me, saying "Here you go. This is what you wanted. I want to give you what you want." I was pissed and hurt. He originally had wanted me to use my lawyer and it was going to be May when we would start the proceedings. I kept him in the loop every step of the way so he would not be surprised. "Now, *now*, you are going to give me what I want! Are you kidding me? just like that. After all these years of being married and the things I wanted during our marriage didn't mean shit to you. Now you are giving me what I want. What the hell is this? This is bullshit." I did not hold back. I didn't even know he had a lawyer, let alone had the papers already drawn up. I was absolutely unprepared for this, what felt like I was sucker punched.

Apparently, Tim wanted to deliver the divorce papers to me himself, not have someone else do it. Understandably he was upset, yet his attitude reflected much of what I had lived with. My instinct and my new established boundaries were taking over. Without a second thought, I firmly stood my ground, and told him in a stern and raised tone of voice, to make sure he could hear me, as he was starting to back out of the parking lot. "Tim, this is why, this right now, how you are," as I waved my hand in front of me in a large circle over and over. "Tim, this is exactly why *I am done*. This is the attitude that you have right now. This is not just about the papers. This attitude of yours is what I have lived with most of our married life and I am tired of it. I am sick of it, and this is why I am done. It is this attitude. It is your attitude."

Tim stepped on the brakes and started to pull back into the parking lot. He looked at me with the saddest eyes and said, "I do not know what else to do!" He started crying and got out of the pickup, repeating, over and over, "I do not know what else to do."

Thinking Tim might pass out as he is wracked with such pain, crying so hard looking, shaking so much, I took him inside and we sat down at the table and we started to talk. We started talking through all this again. Even though Tim had been to three different therapists in the previous five months to figure out for himself how to make this work, nothing had really worked for him.

Even though my whole being was done, I was done, I still loved Tim. I still wanted the best for him. I still wanted happiness for him. I knew that it did not include me in that picture. Everything in me was done with that relationship.

I gave Tim two phone numbers, one of which was for Melvin. I encouraged Tim to call Melvin, who I had worked with in the past. Melvin is an exceptional mentor and coach. I do not know why but that was what came through to me, "give Tim Melvin's phone number." If anyone could help Tim through all of this I knew it was Melvin. After over an hour of talking, Tim was calm enough to drive home.

I sat there holding the divorce papers in my hand. It was now reality. The papers were filed that Friday in April. It was such an odd feeling, one that is hard to put words to. A part of my life was now over, done, no more.

I texted Melvin to let him know, "Hey Melvin, letting you know, Tim gave me divorce papers today. I gave Tim your number to call you, he is really shook up, he may be calling you."

The text message I received back from Melvin, shocked me. "Tammy, you and I need to talk." I felt the sternness in Melvin's text message. "Ummm, ah, Ok," I murmured with a bit of a shocked sound to my voice, staring at my phone, like, what the hell? This wasn't about me it was about helping Tim.

The next day, Saturday, Melvin and I got on the phone and talked for almost four hours. I was in my apartment. He has a unique knack for cutting to the chase and an ability to finish my sentences. He told me, "Tammy, sometimes us men, need a brick building to fall on us to wake us up and sometimes that brick building falling on us will not even do the job. Tammy, you leaving was the brick building Tim needed to hopefully wake him up."

In my apartment, the one place I feel safe, having this conversation with Melvin, I was standing in front of my bathroom mirror and looking at myself. Melvin says to me, "Give me a chance Tammy, just give me a chance. Let me call Tim, let me talk to Tim. Tammy, you know I got your back."

Dammit, Melvin just said the words that God knew I needed to hear, "Tammy, you know I got your back." I started cussing. I was pissed, pissed at God and pissed at Melvin. "Are you fucking kidding me, you really want me to do this again, you really want me to try another time, but I am done dammit, I am done." As I was looking in the mirror, having the pissed off conversation with God, all of a sudden in my mind's eye, I viscerally saw and felt these thick, thick heavy cinder blocks falling away from my heart. One by one, the heavy protection that I had unknowingly built up around my heart was falling away. This was the heaviness that I had carried with me for years, which I am sure started to build up during childhood.

To my amazement, I saw this little itty bitty tinge of light coming through all that thickness and this feeling of hope started to pop through internally. My frightened mind was saying no way, no way, I am done, I'm done I'm done. I had to protect me and my heart. Do you really want me to do that again? There was something bigger and more powerful than me taking control. I could not stop it if I wanted to. The Power of God was at hand within me, and a new part of my soul was peaking through.

That saying I so often heard growing up, "I saw the light," this was a whole new version of it. It was a light after death — the death of what my marriage was, the death of the old relationship. There was a rebirthing happening, something I did not really understand at the time. I was too pissed, which really comes from fear. I was so damned scared to go there again, to open up my heart one more time. I truly thought God and Melvin were absolutely crazy. We tried so many different things and nothing worked for more than foru months at a time. Why now, why this way, what was going to be so special?

Melvin, proposed this to me: "Tammy, let me call Tim. Let me talk to him. Let me see where he is at. Tammy, you know I will tell you the truth. If he is not there then you will know. This way you will know and you will know to move on if that is what it ends up being . If he is there, you give me that chance> Sherrie and I have 100% success rate in helping couples to stay together." In my mind I was thinking, "Bullshit." An internal struggle for my life is going on. Are you kidding me, you really want me to open up to that again, to open my heart up again, are you really kidding me?

There was no time to waste. Melvin called Tim the next day, Sunday, and they talked. Melvin called me back, and proceeded to say, "Tammy, that man loves you so much. He would even sell the farm for you." The farm that is his lifeline, the farm that has been in his family for over five generations. Tim was willing to sell the farm, to give up his lifeline, the one thing that courses through his veins, his family farm, to get me back. Whatever it took he was willing to do.

I confirmed with Tim that he is willing to do the work with Melvin and his wife Sherrie, the Intense one-on-one couple counseling in person, in Beverley Hills. Tim said he was committed to doing this work, and he asked me, "How are we going to pay for this?" I point blank told him, "You are Tim! You are paying for it. You are paying every cent of it. I know what money means to you. If you pay for it all, pay for the entire trip, then I will know you are invested in this because you would not like throwing all that money down the drain."

Tim started showing signs that he was serious about this. He said "yes" to paying for all of it. He asked one of our daughters to help him set up his own email account. That was huge! He didn't like computers, let alone ever want to have his own email account. And then he proceeded to fill out all the questionnaires in full and get them back to Melvin promptly.

Not really knowing what we were getting ourselves into, the five-hour drive to Denver was a bit nerve wracking at times. There were odd feelings and an uncomfortableness that would come and go with both of us. To fly out to Beverly Hills, California, was a pretty big deal for Tim. He doesn't like flying, let alone flying into one of the biggest cities, Los Angeles. We both decided not to rent a car and drive ourselves to our hotel close to Melvin and Sherrie's home. That would have been too much.

Melvin was our "Dr. Phil," saying in his own way, "How's that working for you so far?" Was I setting myself up? Melvin is going to let us know how our ideas have gotten us into this mess and how to correct and continue. What was I, what were we, going to learn about us?

The different signs Tim showed me before our first meeting with Melvin and Sherrie all helped me to see,that Tim was really serious about doing this work of trying to fix our relationship. He was serious enough about it, at the very least about checking it out to see if we had a chance of making things work out. Before we left on the trip, Tim cancelled the divorce paper proceedings. He called his lawyer and told him to cancel it all. That was when I knew, ok, maybe we have a chance here, just maybe.

I had called my lawyer, John, and told him what we were doing. He was ecstatic and wished us both the very best. Seeing Tim make things happen in regards to me and our relationship is what helped me to do more than contemplate the idea of opening up my heart again. It helped me to know and feel on a new level that he really was serious. I started to allow the idea, baby step by baby step, "Hmmm, can this really be the answer? Was Melvin our Golden Goose?"

Even though I was slowly starting to let my guard down, the remembrances of all the times when we tried to make it work before would visit me often, especially over that weekend. Within less than 12 hours we were using the tools Melvin and Sherrie were teaching us. Some so simple I would think, "Why didn't I think of that one!" Yet they were very powerful. I was learning to speak up in the moment of hurt feelings, when something was said and Tim was learning about his tone of voice. Wow. We were making shifts happen really quickly as we worked through different triggers. I remember one moment in particular when we ended up laughing after we had worked through the issue at hand.

Choosing Mother's Day Weekend to meet up with Melvin and Sherrie was easy. There was no second thought about that one. I knew that there was no Mother's Day for me that year, and as devastating as realization that was, I knew that was the weekend to go see Melvin and Sherrie. We needed to get to it as quickly as possible. I still feel the sadness in my heart knowing there was no Mother's Day for me that year, even with the understanding of why it was so.

This was a major life changing event. This was the make it or break it time. Thinking this all through for oneself is a vital step. We needed to decide whether or not this relationship was worth opening up our heart once again, to trying once again, knowing that this was the final chance to make things work.

Sometimes, there is a greater help, a divineness, that finds its way into our heart and mind that helps with this process. That was my personal experience. Sometimes we really do have to have the faith of a mustard seed. This certainly became a true understanding for me as I stepped through this process, as I was about to open my heart again. There is an entire mourning process that happens, mourning what never was, what never will be, the lost time, how it could have been, while at the same time working on building a new relationship — not fixing the old, allowing the old to die, and creating a new more profound and real relationship

Never hide from your feelings, especially the ones some call dark, even negative. Acknowledge those feelings. They have got to have a voice. Allow them to come up. If you feel you cannot share them out loud, s then write about them. These feelings must have a voice and they are relying on you to bring out of your body into acknowledgment. This is truly a part of you.

Know that during this process, it is ok and oh so normal to have the feelings of deep anger, fear, resentment, distrust. I felt a fury unlike anything I had ever known, because I hid it away deeply away, covered it up and not wanting to admit this was inside of me. I certainly did have those feelings. They were there. I wanted to lash out.

Yet, there was something higher and greater that was helping me along, guiding me. At times I wanted to scream at Tim, "Why the fuck did you wait so long? Why the hell did it have to come to this, me leaving, to wake you the fuck up?" These were my honest thoughts.

I didn't know then as I know now, after going through the work we did with Melvin and Sherrie, that my devastating action of leaving had to happen in order to break the paradigm that Tim lived in. For generations, no matter what, no matter how miserable anyone ever was in his lineage, no one ever left. They stuck it out no matter how miserable they were. That is just the way it was. Tim never ever thought I would leave. When I did, *bam*, that broke what he knew and saw and grew up with. Those walls came crumbling down, never to go back up again.

This is why the fact remains that we have got to know that the other side is completely committed, as a requirement to move forward. We have to know with complete confidence that they have commited without hesitation. We have to know by their actions that they are serious about taking this last chance to make things right. It was a breath of fresh air for me when Tim agreed whole heartedly to pay for the all the work, the traveling, all it took to get us to Beverly Hills, to work in person with Melvin and Sherrie. I knew Tim was for real and going to do what it took, at the very least give it a real shot. Having a sign from your partner, actually a few signs, to show that they are really committed to working things through is a must. This is no rolling of the eyes, "whatever" moment. This is when the guts hit the fan, this is the final attempt.

We needed that third party person/couple with us, one that could help both of us through this coming together in a new light, a new mindset. I have been asked personally to be a mediator with relationships both that wanted to work it out and ones that had already split up. Having that third party is vital in my opinion for success to happen.

Now we are saying to tear down the walls and take a chance again. Yes, I know about all those years of building the walls around your heart and mind. It is time. You can do this. You can see that your partner is committed by the actions they are starting to take. Sometimes there is one in the relationship who may be stronger than the other, to really help to get the party started.

This was the foundation of the "Second Start" — both of us committed. There was no turning back, we were in this, together. We were building back up the trust, that foundation of the new relationship. It was the beginning of the Second Start, the basis of it. We had turned the corner. We were both on board and moving forward even though we were both scared. It takes time, it takes consistency, it takes at a continued commitment, it takes scheduling in the calendar for the both us.

CHAPTER 16
Melvin and Sherrie

When I left our home on that Sunday night, November 10, 2013, I knew absolutely in every cell of my being that I was done with my marriage. I had no idea, absolutely none, that six months later I would be driving in a car to Denver with my husband, in order to fly out to Beverly Hills to work on our relationship.

Apprehension, uncertainty, protecting my heart, on high alert — those are some of the feelings that I can actually put into words to describe how I was feeling. I was scared, really scared, and wondering if this really could be the answer to fixing our relationship. I was still getting used to the thought that I was actually considering working on my relationship one more time. I was opening up to that possibility again. I knew God had to be there with us, driving with us. Something extraordinary was easing my gut-wrenching fear of opening myself up to this new possibility, this one last chance. If this did not work, we both knew we would go forward with the divorce.

I had the faith of the mustard seed. It started to grow bit my bit as I kept reminding myself while on our five-hour drive that Tim had to be committed. He is getting on an airplane, which was huge, for someone who does not like to fly, let alone going to a big city. The farm boy was going to the city, and he paid for this all to happen. He was going to meet a man and woman he had barely spoken to, had never met, and he had no idea what to expect.

Neither one of us knew what we were really saying yes to, not in detail. We only knew we were saying yes to trying one more time, that this was our last-ditch effort to keep together a family that loved each other — five children, ten grandchildren and a marriage of over 34 years. And we were going to be working towards making it better.

Melvin came to pick us up at LAX — what a relief. The last thing either one of us wanted to do was to try to figure out how to get to our hotel. We had enough on our minds. Thank goodness Melvin took care of that part. He knew that we did not need that additional stress.

Tim and I both shocked Melvin when he suggested a couple different options: one, he could drop us off at the hotel and we could rest for the day and get started the following day, or we could go straight to their place and get started right away.

Tim and I looked at each other and said, "We are getting started now, no time to waste." I joked with Melvin, "You know me, I do not waste time." Or like what Bo Eason said to me when we were working together, "Damn Tammy, you are a fricken wedge buster. You do not let anything stand in your way of getting the job done. Tammy you are always righting the ship. Do you really know how courageous you are Tammy? Not just anyone opens their heart again not like this."

"Besides, Melvin, we are farmers, we are from the country. We are here to get it done". Tim is also a superintendent of an asphalt crew on major highway construction, and I raised our five kids while Tim was out of town almost eight months of the yea. We both know what it takes to get the job done. We went to Beverly Hills to make shift happen, not to delay and wonder about it. Melvin called Sherrie to let her know we were on our way, we were getting started now! I laughed.

One of the requirements before meeting with Melvin and Sherrie was that we filled out three detailed assessments. I did not know how they would be used or what the benefit would be, yet I trusted Melvin that there was purpose to all of this prep work. The questions that were asked made me delve deep within myself because when I commit to doing this type of work I dive full in. Even though I had filled out questionnaires in the past, this was all new to Tim. One was called The Love Languages, and I had done that one years before, and I also had my children do it so I could learn what their love languages were. It's so odd, but Tim and I both have the same love language, but there are different ways to speak the language to each other, just as there are different dialects, for instance, within spoken languages.

What felt like a huge load of bricks I had been carrying fell from my shoulders when I understood that the work we were doing that weekend was not about fixing the old relationship of 34 years. The work we were doing was about creating a new relationship, and we would move forward from there.

One of the things we were each asked to do is to write down three things we wanted to address, to figure out and to move forward on. My three were put wood flooring in our bedroom, move the deer heads that were mounted on the walls and landscaping. We had talked about the flooring for a number of years but we had never done it. As for the deer heads, hunting deer was one way we fed our family, especially with raising five children on one income for almost two decades. At times, there would be a deer that was beautiful enough to mount, and where it went was on our wall in the living room. I had asked for years for them to be moved out to a different place. As for the landscaping, I wanted to see beauty when I drove up the drive way. It was a requirement for my soul.

My three requests may sound simple, yet they meant a lot to me. I had felt all those years that the simple things that I desired to be done were never important or convenient for Tim. What I asked for was never a priority, and that made me to feel unloved by my husband. My thought was, "If Tim truly loved me then the things I am asking for are simple enough. I am not asking for the moon. If he loved me then I would be at the top of his list and things would get accomplished."

In time I could see that since I grew up with feeling that my wants and needs never mattered to my parents, I was relying on Tim to take care of that hole inside of me. Wow, I never felt important to my parents, and now I feel I am not important to my husband. I realized that that unconscious thought was playing a part in the heartache I had experienced in my married life. Uncovering that thought was priceless. It is as if an unknown burden I had placed on our relationship was starting to lift.

We discussed in depth about the deer heads being on our living room wall. I was as amazed as Tim was at what we discovered. Sherrie gently probed Tim and helped him to dig deep into what the deer heads meant to him. When new people would come to the farm, most of them were amazed at the deer heads and the stories behind each one of them because all five of them were unique, especially Tim's 22-point buck.

We were both a bit in shock when Sherrie helped Tim to understand that the bragging rights that went along with the deer heads were about the ego. They were what made Tim feel important. These were the stories he could tell. That is exactly how he grew up, with his uncles and cousins bragging about the bucks they bagged. You were a man if you had that trophy buck. Tim's worth was judged by his prowess as a hunter and how good at sports he was. Without those two things, he was nothing. That was passed down to Tim by the men on both sides of his family. This is generational in many families, especially when it comes to sports.

Tim started to understand that he was more of a real man when he was taking care of his relationship with his woman than the symbol of a deer head on the wall. As soon as Tim understood this about himself, he was willing to take them down and put them somewhere else. His hesitation about that for all those years was gone. Just as important, I understood why they were so important to Tim; they represented his manhood. No wonder he refused me this one thing I wanted to happen for so many years. Realizing it was not about him not wanting to please me, it made more in a sense. I wanted to take away something that made him feel proud. It was almost like I was threatening his manhood. In a way, without knowing it, by asking him to move the deer heads out of the room, I was actually asking him to take away a part of his identity.

After all this time of thinking the deer heads were more important than me, that feeling diminished, as soon as I also realized in this process that my disappointment stemmed from my childhood feelings of never being important to my dad. Somehow the two were connected. I grew up feeling that football was more important to my dad than I was. I had developed a deep hatred for football, and that too has been healed. This is why it is vital in my opinion to continue the inner work on oneself. Those deep feelings of not being loved followed me into my marriage and were triggered by the fact that Tim would not move the deer heads. I am amazed at how interesting life plays out in so many different ways.

It was such an incredible learning lesson for me, and for Tim as well. You do not need a deer head on the wall to say how much of a man you are. More than that, your relationship is the real trophy that shows how much of a man or woman a person is. Are both people happy and thriving? What a concept! Once I really understood all of this, my grinding desire to get the deer heads off the walls diminished. They no longer represented Tim's lack of care about me and my feelings.

Another thing that I had wanted while living with Tim was a new bedroom set. Tim had also wanted one, and we had talked about it off and on for over a decade, yet we still never bought one. We would buy for our children, but we rarely bought for ourselves. We had never in over 34 years of marriage had anything but secondhand mismatched bedroom furniture. I was tired of it. When I moved out one of the first things I did was go shopping for a new bedroom set to put in my apartment. I felt like a princess the first night it arrived, almost a month later, and pretty much every night since then when I looked at it and slept on it, I felt like the princess who finally received what she deserved.

Tim started to see how easy it actually was to show me love, to make me feel loved. He would beat himself up, shaking his head, look at me and say, "It was this easy to love you and I was too damned hard-headed to see it." Tim so much wanted to show me how much he wanted our relationship to work that he chose to be the one to install the wood flooring in our bedroom.

I realized that, for Tim, that was a major way of working on our relationship. Tim was putting everything into personally pulling out the old, and to him putting the new into our relationship was symbolized by replacing that floor. This was his way of expressing to me, "Tammy, I am committed and determined piece by piece, nail by nail, on my knees (which is extremely uncomfortable for him), to make our marriage work."

Once we saw the finished floor and the new bedroom furniture moved in, he stood there in awe, looked over at me with tears in his eyes and expressed with a new depth of his heart coming to the surface, "Wow, it was this easy to make you happy, this easy to show you how much I love you, and I was too stupid to see it. Damn, why was I so stupid, why was I so damn blind? I never saw how easy it was to make you happy."

Sometimes people love you the only way they know how. It may not be the way you want. If you can open your eyes to see and understand how they are loving you, it can open your heart to new possibilities. It can open a new area of conversation. You start to understand that they really do love you because of their actions.

What is the bedroom floor in your life? Look at one thing that your partner, present or past, did for you, especially if you thought it was about them. Why didn't they do it my way? Why doesn't he get what I am talking about? Those are usually the instances where they are showing love the only way they know how.

Really seeing this helps to ease the disappointment of what you think it should be. Really seeing should ease the discontent that has built up, layer by layer, over the years. It might ease the disappointment of what you are not getting and you have wanted for so long, such as attentiveness, cards, flowers, presents, trips, date nights, incredible love-making.

Once you learn to accept the way they offer their love to you, you can start to have the conversation of "thank-you," the conversation of "gratitude." This helps the other person to realize that you are aware of how they are loving you. Appreciating them for what they are giving helps to open their mind to a new conversation, to new ideas, to what and how to take it a step further.

Let that other person know you see them and their efforts. It helps them to feel that they are significant in the relationship, that they are contributing possibly in the only way they know how for the time being. Then you can open up communications and talk about how you would like the special earrings, the flowers, maybe the new ring that now represents the new relationship. Your requests are more likely to be heard, for now it comes from a more loving perspective and connection.

CHAPTER 17

64 Chevy

It was no magic pill that we received from Mel and Sherrie that Mother's Day weekend in May 2014. Everything wasn't suddenly all better. However, we had a starting point for working on our second start, and we had new tools to help us do the work.

Things were better in the sense that hope was growing. We had belief in the process and an understanding of what was possible if we both worked at creating a new relationship, and not worry about fixing the old one. In a sense we were building a new foundation. Trust and faith were with us as we started walking through the unknown, and we still had the reality of us both wondering if this could really work, when nothing else we had tried before ever had. Those were exciting times, yet also scary.

Opening my heart back up to the possibility of being crushed deep down was terrifying, because I had been down this road before, but I was willing to try this one last time. That in itself was a true miracle to me. God certainly helped get us to the place of starting, but it took doing the work to make the magic happen, to create the miracle.

One of the agreements we made during that intensive weekend with Melvin and Sherrie was that I was going to keep living in my apartment. I still needed that for myself. I was still in healing mode even though I didn't realize it at the time. That that was part of what was going on inside of me. The weekend was not a quick fix , yet it was a tremendous start. I was amazed at all we learned to incorporate into our ways of thinking. Spending time working one-on-one with Melvin and Sherrie would eventually save our marriage. But we had to do the work. There was no way around it.

Tim and I agreed to have a night a week when we would get together. It was tough because Tim was out of town working all week, working up to 14 hour days paving highways in the excruciating heat of the summer, and come home exhausted and still had the farm to take care of. So, making sure he scheduled time for me, for us, making that a priority, stepping up to the plate like that, showed me that he was really committed to making this all work.

My apartment ended up being our haven. We knew we would not be interrupted and it was our space to just be with one another. It gave us the opportunity to get to know each other on new levels with no distractions. The notebooks we came home with from that weekend still stand as a great guideline to follow, and they are still at our fingertips if we ever require a reminder.

Slipping back into old patterns can and does happen. That is part of being human and it is reality. When that happened, we grabbed the notebooks, read, listened, and did some of the exercises. All of that helped us to understand about ourselves and one another in a way that was priceless. We realized things about each other and ourselves that were never obvious before that marvelous weekend of exploration.

Being in dating mode started to put some fun back into our marriage. We took turns making it happen. Again this required Tim to step up and not rely on me to always make a decision and figure this part out. Some of the most enjoyable times were when Tim would call me, ask me out and pick me up in our 64 Chevy convertible. I was so surprised — they were real dates. I couldn't believe it when he told me months later that he got a speeding ticket one of the times because he was running late to come and get me and he just did not want to be late.

The previous year, on a Saturday in October 2013, when I was preparing for the day in a few weeks when I would walk out of our marriage, Tim pulled up in the yard, as proud as ever, showing me the convertible he bought for me. Ever since I was a little girl I had dreamed of owning a convertible and of driving freely in the wind. And now here he was with a 64 Chevy Impala two-door white convertible, beaming with pride, saying, "Hey, look what I got for you, your convertible."

I pretended to be happy for his sake and the sake of everyone standing around. Inside though, I was frustrated and angry and holding back the tears, saying to myself, "Now! Now he does this. Now."

But after hour weekend in Beverly Hills, new feelings started rising to the top. I began to feel gratitude for the convertible as Tim would pull up to my apartment and take me out for the evening, often with no destination in mind. Sometimes we would end up at the Sonic, ordering our Pepsi and onion rings, which brought back memories of when we were first dating over 30 years ago.

We were having fun enjoying each other and being free. It felt really good to be on this new path with each other, starting to trust in what we were working on. We were still scared, wondering if what we were doing was going to work. But making time for fun was essential in the process of it all and it still is. Having fun together at something we both enjoyed was a vital component to creating the glue that would help cement our new foundation together. We were building upon Joy, laughter, giggles and fun moments. What better way to bring back together two broken-hearted souls who deeply wanted the best for each other and their family. We had so much at stake and we both knew it. Lightening up the situation with fun times was one of the best things we did. We made sure to schedule in those fun times, intentionally figuring out what could we do together that was fun. This was a pivot that helped us along the way. Fun togetherness had diminished in our marriage to the point of non-existence. Oh, I was fun and made sure I had fun in my life. However, as a couple, that tap had dried up.

In time we started to involve our family in the process, going to pick up some of the grandkids, taking them for a ride in the convertible. Tim seeing the smile on my face, hearing me giggle with glee like I was one of the kids, helped him to know that he was doing something right. That was one of his fears, making sure he did something right for us, with me, wanting so much for our relationship to work out and for me to say yes to moving back to the farm.

I stayed living in my apartment for an additional eight months after Tim and I went to go see Melvin and Sherrie that Mother's Day weekend in 2014. It was where I felt safe. It may have only been 800 square feet, but it was more than just an apartment to me. It was my Goddess domain, where healing myself was happening on many levels, some of which I did not know existed.

My apartment was my sanctuary, my sacred space, and no one entered without my permission, and all understood this. I now had "my space." I did not have to share it with anyone.

I had never realized how vitally important that was for me. Raising five children, losing myself in the process, I never knew that I had a choice to create boundaries. I never realized I was not setting boundaries in those early days of my life. I was learning that while living on my own. Wow, people had to have my permission to enter. Ha, what a new concept for me.

My apartment was like a womb, where I felt safe, nurtured and taken care of. Possibly that was because that it was what I was doing for myself in that apartment, and I had never done before in my life, not like this. It was all about me, what fed me, what I desired. For the first time in my life, I was really able to concentrate on me and my needs and wants and dreams. Naturally I would miss her when I eventually did move out.

When Tim would show up for date night, it meant to me that he had made the effort. He made the effort to think about what he was going to wear, to come to town, to spend money on the extra gas he was now using to come to see me. He respected my apartment, taking his boots off at the door as I asked him to do. Something that seems so little as taking off your shoes was actually big to me. It was a sign of respect for me and showed me that what I wanted, even if it seemed so minor, was being heard. I was being heard. I was being listened to, and my wishes were being respected.

I learned to start saying yes to me more, nurturing and healing myself, to the point of saying a true no to other things. I was no longer allowing the feeling of obligation to rule my life. If I needed some time to myself I would say, a "thank-you and no," even to my kids and my grandkids, missing a soccer game or two along the way. The healing of me, my soul, my heart and mind, took top priority. It had to. I was no good to anyone else if was I was no good to and with my own self.

I really encourage you, if you ever go through something of this degree, to create your own space. You deserve it, even if it is a corner in your bedroom. I understand if you cannot afford to move out on your own, and some do not want to go to that extreme. However, there are times when it is necessary to have our own space in order to make shifts really happen. Honestly, why wait until something major happens, create it now.

Having your own space, your go-to space, whether it is an apartment or just an area where you currently live, that is where you start to heal at deeper levels. It is a place where you write, think, read and most importantly, *just be with you.* If there is one thing I can recommend without hesitation, it is the importance of your own space — your sanctuary for you. I highly encourage you to really consider what space you have right now, whether or not you are having issues in your relationship. Right now, look around and figure out how you can make yourself some precious space — even if you have to make your space your bathroom for an hour.

This is about you, for you. It is up to us to take care of ourselves. When you create your own space and treat it as a sacred space, and you sit in it, be in it, you also are telling your soul, your body, your mind and spirit that you are sacred. It is time. I invite you to start treating yourself as such no matter what is going on in your life. You are enough! You are worthy! You are deserving! You Are Sacred!

CHAPTER 18
New Floor

The creation of the new relationship Tim and I were embarking on had three conditions from each of us, which were discussed, understood and agreed upon before we left Melvin and Sherrie. I talked about my three conditions in Chapter 16. They were things that never seemed to be important enough to make Tim's list of priorities. These three things were what I asked for in order for me to truly know and feel that Tim was committed to me and our relationship before moving back to the farm. My three things were not about me only; they were things that would eventually feed both of us.

Tim and I had talked for years about replacing the old carpeting in our bedroom with hardwood flooring, it was something we both wanted, yet there was always something else more important. When was it going to be my time? This Is a question that I asked throughout our marriage.

I was so so so tired of looking at the deer heads hanging on our wall in the front room. I wanted art to cover the walls not dead deer heads.

I love to have beauty around me, and not just the inside of our home. I had been wanting again for years to have our yard landscaped, not the entire yard, but a part of it. I just wanted to see beauty in our yard, when I drove up. I was tired of seeing the blah of things. We didn't water our grass because we were on a well and we lived on a farm. You saved your water for yourself and your livestock. I could never get it through Tim's head how much better our home would look if we had some beautiful landscaping in front of it. I understood that this could not happen until the following spring, but I appreciated the fact that we were discussing it, that I was not being dismissed or made to feel stupid because of something I wanted.

Tim had agreed to all three of my requests. He finally understood in some respects why he was always ignoring my requests, especially in regards to the deer heads.

The bedroom floor was the most important to me. Later on I would find out how really significant it was. Something in me the woman, the girl, the teenager and more, started to heal at levels I did not understand at the time. And I certainly did I not know they were there to the degree they were until Tim took the first step when he said to me, "Let's go shopping!"

"For what?" I asked, with a puzzled look on my face. "Let's go shopping" is not at all something that Tim would say out of the blue. Such a comment would normally have me going over to put my hand on his forehand, all in fun, and see if he had a fever. He wanted to go shopping to look for our new wood flooring. I was ecstatic to say the least! He was doing it. He was taking the initiative and making it happen. The pressure was off of me — phew! There was to be no reminding him, nudging him, dropping hints, something I am sure many of us women do, hoping that the man will get it. And of course we set ourselves up for disappointment when they do not get it.

The fact was that something important to me was now important to Tim. It really felt good, oh my gosh, it felt so good. This was incredibly huge for me, that something I wanted, something we had talked about for years was finally going to happen. Putting a wood floor in may sound simple. Oh, just hire someone to do the work, you may think, yet that is not how Tim thinks, especially, if he can do the work himself. The fact that Tim took it upon himself to ask me to go shopping, taking that first step was huge for me and our relationship.

Replacing the floor was one of those things that I required help with. It required joint decision-making because there are too many factors involved to complete this particular job on my own. Now, with Tim taking the initiative, I was starting to feel important to him. I always knew in my head I was, but my heart had to feel it for it to be real, and there was no way around that. I now know that about myself, and I no longer deny that aspect of me. I used to ask God, "Why can I not feel in my heart of hearts?" It was as if there was a block in me that I could not understand.

Do you remember the cinder blocks that I shared with you a few chapters ago? I had unknowingly built up those protective blocks around my heart in order not to be hurt as deeply.

When you love deep, you hurt just as deeply.

Tim taking charge, telling me with love that we are going shopping meant so much to me. Finally I was not the one in charge of this one thing. With raising five kids starting at the age of 17 and pretty much always in charge, it felt so damn good for Tim to take the reins. This was one area where I could relax. *Just relax Tammy, Tim has this one handled.* I felt comfortable, protected and safe, what I always wanted.

When Tim started paying attention to my requests, and more importantly, started acting on them, that is when I started to believe in him and in us for the first time in a very long time. When I saw him working on the floor in the bedroom, it was as if with every piece of wood he laid down, which he was doing with so much care and love, he was taking down the cinder blocks that had built up around my heart. It was this I had to see. I had to see Tim take so much care in doing this work. It was not about saving money — doing the work on the floor himself was the way he knew how to work on our relationship. It was his gift to me and even more to himself.

It did not matter that Melvin told me, "Tammy, he loves you so much and wants you back, he would sell the farm for you." "Whatever, ok fine," I thought. Or my kids saying, "Mom, Dad is all broke up about you leaving, he wants you back." Or Tim telling me, "Tammy, I love you so much. How can we make this work?" None of those words got through to me. What mattered was that Tim had heard me, really heard me, and he translated what I wanted into action. His actions were disassembling the dam that had been holding back my emotions, my ability to feel him and his love for me.

It was the *action* that Tim was doing that started to break down the walls to my heart. It was important that *he* Initiated the action. His deeds are what started to break down the barriers. Tim was paying attention to my wants and needs, realizing in the process that deep down, they were really so simple.

The saying "actions speak louder than words" was true in our relationship, which was vital for me because that is my love language, "acts of service."

He was like at kid at times with his love and enthusiasm. Laying the floor was his way of rebuilding our relationship, and it was a perfect metaphor — piece by piece, one by one being securely stapled into place, building the everlasting foundation. There were a few mistakes made, some not noticed until several pieces had been laid. Taking them up to redo them correctly was a pain in the butt, but it was necessary. Did he like to do it? No. Did it take longer then? Yes. Was it worth it in the end? You better believe it! Think about this: some situations have us going back for a redo so we can get it right.

The same goes with our own relationship. There are times when we have to stop, correct and then continue. Even when we do not want to take that extra time and attention, it is so worth it in the end, because the lasting result is incredible. It will shine brighter than ever.

Every single board in that floor was touched with love, and that energy of love is the foundation that our bed now sits on. Every time we walk into our bedroom, our sacred space, we are reminded of the agreement we made to commit to our second start.

Believe me, I understand what I am about to suggest to you. I implore you to open up your mind and your heart to see your partner working hard on your relationship, even if it is not the way you think it should look. Allow a whole new meaning to surface. It helped me to realize of some of things that were going on inside of me. It made Tim realize how easy it was to make me happy. Tim wanted and needed direction, and I never knew that. I had the view that "he should know." My mindset started to change even more. Tim was now open to hearing what my needs are. He wanted direction.

The process of me leaving our home opened him up to accepting and receiving that direction, as well as attempting to find the way on his own, for example, by initiating the shopping trip. I realized that although the way he showed his love was not the way I necessarily wanted, that did not mean it was not a way. Open yourself up to different possibilities and allow your partner to show you love in their own way.

Understanding and accepting that part of them helps to open them up to *hearing you* when you give gentle suggestions of what you desire even more, like a bouquet of flowers, or help putting up Christmas lights, or sitting down with you and the grandkids to play a card game. You may be surprised at how your partner will start to come around when you also start to take those actions that make them feel filled up.

When we get out of our own conceptions of what we think the relationship should look like, the possibilities are endless. Let go of what TV, magazines, books, stories have told you and allow yourself to open to the new of what can be. When we allow our partner to show us love in their way, we open up new areas of healing for them, which is just as important as our healing.

This kind of allowing really can be an aphrodisiac. I am serious. I spilt some milk in the fridge one day, and I was frustrated that I had to start cleaning out the fridge, drawer by drawer. Out of the blue Tim started to help. Wow, I felt so incredibly loved by his *action*, which turned a frustrating situation into a loving and fun time. Tim thought I was a bit nuts when I told him how much him helping was turning me on and that I wanted to make love right there on the kitchen floor. I was totally hot for him in that moment. I was feeling safe with him, as he had reached out to help me in my time of need. He was easing the tension of the situation. This was a new experience for me, and I was loving it and yes even surprised how much my body was reacting to it.

He had reached out with his action, and there was no underlying agenda. He was there totally present in helping me. I felt his presence. I felt him with me. He was not worrying about the different things on his list to do. Life was shining brightly. Relationships are a dance, but unlike old-style dancing, we need to take turns leading.

CHAPTER 19

Take Care of Yourself

The bedroom floor was going in, though not as fast as we thought it would. We both forgot to factor in the fact that Tim worked out of town during the week and only had weekends until around November, when it got too cold to lay down asphalt for road construction. Then there was trying to keep the date nights intact. He only really had Saturday evenings when he could stay home and work on the floor so he could get it done for me to move back into our home — in a way a new home, at least bits and pieces of it would be.

We wanted to start as fresh as we possibly could, and the replacement wood flooring in the bedroom was a significant symbol of that. Actually, it was not even wood; it was even better — bamboo. That too was significant because Tim, a wood lover, agreed to invest in the bamboo flooring we found. For me bamboo had a bigger significance. Bamboo is stronger than wood and it is also flexible and grows a solid foundation for years before it starts to shoot up. It was another great metaphor for our relationship, and I could feel it was a gift from God with the way we found it. I know that God's hand had blessed it and She was waiting for us to discover the source to be able to purchase it.

We continued to work on the homework Melvin and Sherrie gave us, which was out of Tim's comfort zone, so he was stretching himself with that to some degree. However, Tim's commitment to the installation of the floor and wanting to do it all solo, actually needing to do it all on his own, was his personal therapy for himself.

The work we did as a couple also required the personal work we did on ourselves, in order to heal the pain of our hearts, minds and souls. I really feel that was what was so significant for Tim with putting in the bedroom flooring.

Keeping my apartment was my personal therapy. It was a place where I had my Tammy time, which I did not have to share with anyone. It was for me and only me and I felt safe. I was learning how to set better boundaries and stick to them, and my apartment was helping me to do just that. Honestly, I still miss her at times, especially now as I share this. She was a nurturing womb for me, which I feel every woman needs to have in her life, to continue the nurturing of ourselves, no matter where we are in life.

I was learning for the first time in my life at the age of 51 how important it was. I had thought it was selfish to take care of myself, and now I know it is vital and selfless to do so. No woman ever told me this, not to the degree that it really set into me. I was experiencing taking care of myself for myself, and it was life giving.

Eventually, I started to go visit Tim at the farm instead of Tim always coming to see me. I could see, more importantly feel, how important I was to him. Feel is the operative word. You will remember me sharing earlier that during most of our married life, I never really felt that I was important, that I was loved by him. So now, the love was starting to grow, and I was feeling it in my heart and soul. It was not all fireworks because it really was a bit scary. I was not used to feeling. With that new feeling, some of the smaller things started to go by the wayside for the bigger picture.

Over time I noticed, with quite a bit of surprise, that the need to move the deer heads out of the living room dissipated; my tolerance for them grew. How could that be, I would ask myself. I was starting to feel how much Tim was loving me by effort he was putting into the bedroom floor, and I was paying attention to how much he had to juggle in order to also spend quality time with me while working fulltime out of town and having farm work to take care of on the weekends. All this made it obvious to me: I am more important to Tim than the deer heads hanging on the wall.

I also started to ask myself, "What is the big deal with the deer heads, Tammy?" Now that the emotions of the past had dissolved quite a bit, I could see through a different set of eyes, with a more open heart. It was not the deer heads; it was what they represented. I even remember saying one time, "Well, I hope they keep you warm in bed, because I won't be." Dammit, I only wanted Tim to listen to me, to hear me, to do something for me that was not his normal behavior, to do something for me because he loved me that much. Voilà — the flooring.

Because I was really getting it that I was the most important thing to Tim, I started feeling the desire to give back to him, to cut him some slack. So, about once every two weeks, I would go to the farm so he could work on the floor, and also so I could get used to being back there again, as it had been about a year since I has moved out. When I would go visit him at the farm, and end up spending the night, easing me back into the fact that I would be moving back eventually the way things were progressing, we slept in a different bedroom. Things got quite comical at times. We were sleeping on our first bed, my mom's frame and mattress set that we used when we first got married, with the bad mattress. Yes, we still had that bed as one of our kids had used it. There was no buying brand new; we just didn't do that, and we had kept it in their old bedroom. There we were giggling in the makeshift spare bedroom, with just enough room for the double bed shoved up against the wall, with the dresser and all the totes in there with Tim's stuff allowing for a narrow walkway.

Chase, our grandson, aged eight, who grew up living at the farm with his mom, our daughter Crystal, was thrilled to see me on Sunday mornings at the farm, knowing I must have spent the night. Our grandchildren were really affected by me leaving, and Chase probably felt it the most when I moved out. He was so excited to see me in the house right away when he woke up, not coming up the driveway to visit. I could see the gleam in his eyes; his grandma, his sanctuary was back. All the other grandkids were also delighted to see me there to as they started to arrive later that Sunday for dinner.

I talked to our grandkids about what is going on, letting them know that we were dating again. I was always open with them, answering their questions when they would arise, allowing them to talk about their feelings, validating what they felt. My relationship changed with some of them, and now three years later, it is getting back to where I can say each and every one of them is feeling close and safe with me again. It took time though, and at times it was heartbreaking. Yet, as I have shared before, knowing this, I would still do it all over again, because it gave our entire family incredible gifts. The way I see it, miracles happened and still are to this day.

It was not just our conditions that were keeping me from moving back to the farm home. It was also the practicality of life. It was not all rainbows and unicorns, not sure if it will ever be that. What I was sure of though, at that point in time, was that we were both committed and we knew we needed a place for the bedroom furniture we would be moving in to the bedroom. We both desired our bedroom flooring to be done so we could set it all up in there on the day we chose to start moving me back. Life does get in the way at times. Tim thought he could get the floor done in a month, and over three months later, he was still working on it.

Even though we were moving along in our relationship very well, and Tim and I both thought we were on target, we both still had hesitation. There were still the "what ifs" that came up in our minds. There was still that underlying uneasiness. Could we really believe this was working? It is scary sometimes to believe in the good things that are happening; it is human nature. In a relationship that you have been disappointed in so much over the years, was it ok to start believing in that again? I wanted to believe, but there was still a holding back a bit.

When I realized I was believing and believing and believing, and my heart was starting to open back up even more to the grand possibilities of everything — ahhh, the warning bells would go off in my head. Maybe I am believing too much too soon, so pulling back a bit happened naturally.

I had gone to quite an extreme to move out on my own. Trying again was no small potatoes, as the saying goes. This a huge deal, creating a new relationship, depending on the other to keep their part of the bargain. To tear the walls of the dam down was not a simple or easy task.

What if Tim quits working on the floor? What if Tammy says after all this work Tim has done that she chooses not to move home after all? We both still had that little part of us that was a bit scared, scared to believe whole heartedly. We talked about it. Wow! We talked about it. What a new concept in our relationship, and wow, did that ever feel good, to talk it out and to know that we were both feeling it. Even with admitting our fears, we continued to move forward.

Eventually we found out that we were not alone with the cautious feelings. All five of our children felt the same way. What if dad screws up? What if dad cannot meet mom's standards? What if mom's expectations are too high? Will mom give dad another chance if he does mess up? Admitting to those fears and talking about them, sharing them with one another, was vital for the well being of our entire family. And all of our relationships to started to heal on a new level. For belief in something new to be created, there has got to be, without reservation, open communication, no matter how scary that is.

No matter what though, one of the most important things to always keep in mind, is to take care of yourself. That was the most important thing for me. As long as I stood in my truth and took care of myself on all levels, I was more able to get through the fact that my children were angry with me. Some were really pissed off that I left to begin with, and some remained angry even knowing that I was working it out with their dad.

I only had myself to really rely on, and that was why it was important that I kept my apartment and kept learning to take care of myself and my needs. I kept coming back into my feminine essence, my personal care, getting into a routine that eventually I would take home with me and keep up. And if I fell off track, then I would get back on track faster than I would have in the past. It might only take me days instead of weeks or months.

Give yourself some slack, but continue to take care of yourself so you never fall back into depending on someone else to do it for you. You no longer need to blame the other person if things are not working out the way you want them to or thought they should.

As things start to progress and you start to feel this coming together with you and your partner, if for some reason your partner does not meet the expectation of a thought or a wish that you have, you do not get as disappointed as you did in the past. You have a new-found confidence that has grown. You are more dependent upon yourself and not as much on the other person. You accept that even if the other person is trying, and if you are trying, there are still some 'oopses' in a relationship.

Also, whether you are female or male, when you take care of yourself, you actually become more attractive to the other. No one wants a weak person, especially a woman. For me anyway, I need to know that I have a strong man beside me who has my back.

Get used to taking care of yourself because it is important for the new you in your second start. That is how you are going to live your life from now on. Get used to taking care of yourself because that is what life is about now. Taking care of yourself helps build a stronger relationship because you are in a different place in this relationship. This makes you a better person to move forward.

Your partner sees the new you, taking care of yourself, and starts to have a new understanding of who you are and what is important to you. They will possibly start taking care of themselves better. When that happens, it becomes a beautiful win for the both of you.

Your partner starts to see that you are standing up for yourself, for what you want and need. So, as you come back together, there is a new understanding of who you are and what you require to have from your partner.

Think about it, who do you like hanging around with? Most people like to associate with a person who is strong, which does not mean being dominant all the time. It means the person has a certain strength and a certain confidence. That is how a healthy relationship is. I believe the man also needs to know that his woman is strong when he needs her to be, and by taking care of yourself you show him that. It makes you more attractive to your partner in more ways than one.

CHAPTER 20

Ask Me

The New Year of 2014 was upon us, the floor was getting done, and the time was drawing nearer to when I would be moving back to our farm home. "What date do I say no more to my apartment and yes to me living back at the family farm?" This was the question that was going round and round in my mind.

This move back had to be memorable and significant. It was another way of me saying "yes" to my marriage and my commitment to making it work. In my mind, it had to be very special. I didn't want to just pack everything up and bam, I'm back at home. It had to have some planning as I wanted the process to have a special significance.

I also wanted Tim to asked me to move back, not to just assume that I would since we were working on our marriage and yes, I did agree to moving back. There was that one more extremely important step. I had to share with Tim that I needed that step for me. I wanted Tim to ask me, "Tammy, will you move back home and be my wife again?"

I realized that the reason behind this need was that I was never asked when I was pregnant at 17 whether I would marry Tim. It was assumed we would get married and we did. I never had that official proposal. It was a missing link in our relationship.

I wanted to bring it into the now and correct it. I wanted to feel whole in our relationship as we were starting yet another aspect of our second start. It would help to make up for what I missed out on the first go around.

I pondered how I was going to tell Tim this one. Would he understand what I required deep within me? I found it interesting how nervous I was before sharing with him my true feelings and how much it would mean to me for him to ask me to move back instead of assuming I would. I wanted to break the mold, that cycle we had started when we first knew I was pregnant. No more assuming. I wanted to feel significant to him. It is all about feeling for me this second time around, and it was up to me to make sure that the "feel" part stayed at the forefront of our relationship, because the lack of that is what took us down, took me down. The second start was about *feeling the love.*

As we were sitting on the couch and both knew it was coming to that time, I didn't want the assumptions of 30 years ago. This was another way of changing an outcome, creating something new that would be memorable. Have you ever heard that saying, "It takes five good things to erase one bad thing"?

I knew that I required Tim to ask me to move back, and I needed to hear it from his heart, for him to sink into his heart so my heart could connect. I was nervous because I was not sure how he would take it, yet another step that Tammy is asking for. Here I was going again into unchartered territory. I shared with Tim what had been on my mind, and at first, he was totally surprised and unprepared for what I had just said, to the point that he went silent. I felt this energy of, "What the hell? Where did this come from?"

We were still in the process of getting used to the new parts of each other — me really sharing what and how I desired to feel his love, and Tim hearing me on a whole new level and frightened that if he didn't do it all correctly, I would leave again. It did not matter how much I reassured Tim that I was here for the long haul, he still had that fear. As Tim sat there on the couch in silence, I could literally hear his brain attempting to compute what I just laid upon his lap to digest and come up with the proper solution.

Gently, I got up and did things around the apartment for about an hour or so, in order to give Tim more time to think about things. I left him alone to help him calm his nerves and process this information and make sure he felt no pressure from me.

As I went back to sit on the couch with Tim, he reached out to me, took my hand and, with a soft voice with a bit of cracking to it, he said my name, while putting his hand under my chin to gently have me look at him. He looked deep into my eyes and asked me, "Tammy, would you do me the honor of moving back to the farm with me? I want you back at the farm, Tammy. I love you so much." Feeling the depth of his words, our hearts connected on another new level.

Giving Tim time to process was an important step that I grew to know better and better in time. It was something I had never realized in all those years of being together. Realizing this for both Tim and I was one of the top things we learned together when working with Melvin. I was understanding why I had felt so much of the time during our marriage that I was talking to a brick wall. Bam ... a light bulb went off. Melvin would remind me that Tim's mind worked differently, and it was up to me to learn it. I could still hear Melvin's words, explaining to me how Tim's mind did not work the same as mine.

I learned to tell myself, "Back off a bit Tammy. Release the pressure Tammy. Allow him to process Tammy." I was learning how to communicate even better. I could feel the gears in Tim's brain processing all that I shared, trying to figure out the best way for him to say it so it meant something to me, so it would be more than just words.

Both of us were still in a bit of a uncomfortable situation, but our dedication carried us through. A relationship is about two people, not just what I want. It was not just about training Tim to act the way I wanted. It was also about training myself, working on understanding, especially with receiving new insight, how the other person clicks. Too much pressure can shut the other person down. When the other person goes silent, it does not always mean that they are not listening. It may mean that they are processing and attempting to do so as fast as they can to keep up with all that you are putting on them, sharing with them.

Understanding each other and opening ourselves up to new levels of understanding, especially when we seek help, will give you so much more to work with in order to have a relationship that does more than survive. It will give you a relationship that thrives.

To continue the metaphor from the last chapter, a relationship is a dance. Giving some slack and meeting part-way means that sometimes he leads and sometimes I lead. I guide in some directions and then allow him to guide me in other directions. Some of those moves are significant and life altering, and with some moves, we glide through together with ease and grace. Discussing and choosing together the date for me to put in my 30-day notice for leaving my apartment was one of those moments of ease and grace. Sure, I could have put in my notice sooner, saving a bit of money, yet deciding the day would be January 26, 2014, our 34th wedding anniversary, held major significance.

Just as important, if not more so, was allowing Tim ask me in his own time to move back home. It means so much more when it comes from the heart, and not from pressure. It created a new level of connection. I really had to look at myself, as we all should do, and see where my responsibility lay in our relationships. It was my responsibility to share what I desired, what would really help me to feel loved, and not expect the other person to know it. Sometimes it even requires repeating it. No one is perfect. Would we like them to know without saying so? Sure, that would make it so much easier. That is not always reality. Now knowing and being aware of how I can tend to overwhelm helps me to communicate with Tim in a more loving, clearer way, and helps me to think through the importance of some requests.

"Tammy, I really want you to move back, back to our home."

"YES and thank you for asking."

How is that for an ending? If you don't cry you are not alive.

CHAPTER 21
The Rough Spot

After I moved out of our home on November 10, 2013, that year for Christmas, Tim worked with our daughter Crystal, to string lights on both sides our 300-foot driveway. He invested hundreds of dollars to make it happen for the first time.

Tim knew how much I cherished the Christmas season. Growing up, it was the one time that really meant a lot to me. There was always so much love in the air, and everyone was getting along — my mom and dad were no longer fighting. Yet it took Tim until I moved out to make such a huge effort over Christmas. Instead of scowling at the thought of all the lights being put up, he stepped up big time and, with Crystal's help, created an amazing Winter Wonderland on the farm. Even though I had moved out, I was still invited out for Christmas, and as I drove up to the house, all those lights were stunning.

Honestly though, it was somewhat bittersweet. I was in awe, yet I was mad and sad and hurt that it took me moving out for Tim to wake up, to do something so incredible for me. I found out later that he had actually initiated this; it was his idea. It really was so simple to make me happy. That gesture in itself would have been enough of Christmas present for me. It could have been the perfect gift, yet at that time, if you remember, "I was done" with our marriage.

Two years later, Christmas 2015, I had been living back at the farm for nearly a year, and things had been going really well. We were doing great on our second start, continuing to grow and develop our new relationship. With the festive season approaching, I started to put out subtle hints about the lights going back up down the driveway, with comments here and there about the weather and what days would be nice to make it happen.

It was not happening. It was not getting done. Even though things were really wonderful in our new relationship, my antennas were still up. It was still new and fresh, and my guard had not completely gone down.

Tim had made this huge effort just after I moved out, 2 years before, attempting to win me back, by not just investing in more lights, but also in helping Crystal put them up. That action was totally out of character. That was a new Tim breaking through and attempting to show me just how deeply he really cared about me and so much desired to make me happy.

I was starting to feel as if things were slipping back to the old "take me for granted" days. It was not as much about the lights as it was about the initiative he took without me saying anything. It was the fact that it was his idea to put the lights up the whole length of the driveway. He knew how important it would be to me. Now, two years later, it was as if now he couldn't be bothered. It was as if other things took priority over me now that I was back in the home.

It sucks when you keep telling yourself, "I have time, I have time" to get done whatever you have on your to-do list and suddenly your time runs out. I guess Tim was trying in his own way. He initiated a shopping trip, taking me to a jewelry store, and it was not the day before Christmas. That part was an improvement, as it was not totally last minute. It was over a week in advance. After looking at bracelets and then earrings, and going back and forth between the two, I picked out the earrings I wanted. They were not in stock and had to be ordered and the store would call to let Tim know when to come and pick them up.

It was almost Christmas Day and Tim let me know the jeweler had not called him. I suggested that Tim follow up and either make a phone call or go there in person the next time he was in town. Tim never called them or went in. You always follow up, right? No matter the situation, you follow up, whether it is personal or business.

What was happening here? Tim was allowing life to get in the way again, and I was slipping off of his list of priorities. That was how I was feeling. Now that I was back, he was getting too comfortable. He was slipping back to his old ways of being and acting. This was not a time, especially at Christmas, to get lazy about our relationship.

Waking up Christmas morning in bed together, Tim looked at me, and said, "Merry Christmas," then took a deep breath and said, "I know I screwed up!" I looked at him and with a very calm voice said, "Tim, you didn't just screw up. No, you fucked up. I still love you, but you really fucked up, and this time you are the one that needs to make it better." I was amazed at how well I was taking it, with a no-crying-over-spilled-milk attitude. I calmly voiced my feelings. "This one is on you. Now it is up to you to fix this. Figure out a way. I am not saving you from this. You know there is always Melvin to call if you require help. By the way Tim, our anniversary is coming up. Maybe you can make it up then."

I shared exactly how my heart was feeling. I did not mince words. I was not making light of how I felt. I was not brushing it off and sweeping it under the rug, like I used to, and like so many other women I have seen and know about do. I have worked with many of them in my coaching business, and then they walk around with a chip not just on their shoulder but in their heart.

Discussing clearly and sharing exactly how a situation and experience has affected you is very important. Do it with a calm voice — it is important that there be no yelling. I feel it allows the other person to hear you, at least to some degree. I felt so much better when sharing my truth with Tim at how I really felt and not making light of the situation. More importantly, I was not doing it to make him feel bad, but to really have him hear me. This was never to be repeated, not as long as we were together, and he had to know that. He had to really know that I meant business when it comes to him stepping up and making things happen where and when they need to.

I knew he is better than this, and our relationship deserves the best of both of us. He had to know he was responsible and would be held accountable for pulling his own weight in our relationship. I expect the same thing of him to me. I require to know when I am slacking and need to pick it up a notch or two.

Now that I was back at home he could not quit working on the relationship. You don't get lazy and quit doing what is important to the other person. In our old relationship, there was too much laziness and taking for granted.

I kept thinking that maybe he would make up for it on our anniversary, which was only 30 days away. During the time between Christmas and our anniversary, I felt we were just plodding along. Tim started to sleep on the couch in front of our little portable fireplace. Tim was closing down. I was not feeling close to him or loved by him. Things were slipping away. Our anniversary night was blah, just a usual restaurant meal. There nothing to make up for the lack of Christmas lights down the driveway and the lack of present. He was not initiating anything, so again I picked up the slack and started the conversation.

When we started talking, after I asked him why he was not sleeping in our bed, he told me that he needed time to think about things. He had been thinking, "Maybe I need to let her go. I've just got to let her go. Maybe I can't do this. I can't meet all of her expectations."

Have you ever had one of those moments where you are grateful someone shared their thoughts and feelings with you, yet hearing them really pisses you off? That is where I was at, hearing those words. It takes everything you've got to hold on and keep talking through it. Internally, I was pissed at hearing these words, and I finally started to say out loud the thoughts that were going through my mind. Again without raising my voice, and let me tell you, there was a lot of deep breathing through this one, I said "There is no way in hell you are giving up on this. I did not move back in the farm home, I did not let down my walls, I did not open my heart back up, to hear you say, 'I'm done.' No way, this is not happening."

What the hell was going on? What now?

CHAPTER 22
Get Back On

Was I responsible in any way for this happening, the big glitch we were now experiencing? I needed to figure out where my responsibility was in all of this. It always takes two in a relationship. After calling a friend of mine, my no-filter, go-to person, and talking the situation through with her — there it was. I had not been not clear in my communication. I was leaving hints about putting up the lights. I was not clearly expressing my desires and needs to Tim. I was expecting him to read between the lines.

If there is anything I have learned through all of this, it is about how we need to be clear and concise with our communicating. And that applies not just when we want something done, but also when we give a compliment. Yet even though I had learned the importance of clear communication, I too had slipped back into old patterns, and I never realized it in the moment. I cannot expect Tim to hear me when I leave subtle messages. That was the old way, thinking he would pick up on the hints I was leaving here and there. *Is he listening? Oh, he is if the lights get up.* This really is such an unfair way to communicate, and it does no good for your relationship. Quit expecting the other person to know what is on your mind, and start voicing what it is you really desire to share.

Once we take not only responsibility but also accountability for our actions and lack thereof, wow, how our own world can really change and start to transform into more joy. We needed a call with Melvin. Dammit, I hated to admit my part in all of this. For weeks leading up to this point, I kept thinking it was all Tim and he was the one not pulling enough weight in our relationship. I knew we could not fix this one on our own. I was still a bit shocked by what Tim shared with me, telling me he was thinking about letting me go. Here is the thing: I realized why that comment triggered me so much. I grew up never feeling important to anyone, and in my mind my husband was supposed to make me feel important, even lay down his life for me. He was supposed to fight for our relationship, not just passively let it go.

With this realization, I understood more about myself and how my internal workings were playing out in our marriage. I was seeing where I required to look inside of myself and heal those different aspects that were hurting, not so much from Tim but from my own childhood. Tim's actions were what brought them up to the surface.

I knew more than ever, after going to our usual steakhouse for our anniversary, that we needed a Melvin call to get back on track. I was sitting there, in the restaurant, thinking, "What the hell is going on? Why did I come back?" The towel could have really been thrown in for the very last time in that moment, by both of us. All this happened within about six weeks. It sure didn't take long. We had been working for over 18 months on our second start, developing our new relationship. I sure did not expect for the two of us to fall so hard and so quick into the pit of marriage trouble. We were going backwards and fast.

I did not want to be in that restaurant with Tim, and again I am seeing that I did it. I did not share my true feelings with Tim. I should have told him I did not want to go out for our anniversary. I was pretending again things were ok and they were not. Actually, I was allowing Tim to pretend also, by going with him to supper without saying anything, without standing up and speaking my truth.

That night, when we got home and Tim told me he was thinking about letting me go, I told him, "I am calling Melvin, and we are talking about this." There was no choice in the matter. Someone had to take the initiative, and it had to be me at this point in time. "Quit fucking letting life happen and pick up the damn slack," is what I wanted to yell at Tim. He was supposed to be the guy that fixed things, dammit.

I was pissed that it was up to me again. I was angry and hurt. When the going got tough, my partner does nothing, goes into a shell, instead of pulling up his big boy briefs and getting back into it, even if he did not know how. Oh, but he did know how. He knew that Melvin was always there for both of us. That was made very clear.

The next day we were on the phone with Melvin. He had heard the urgency in my voice when I called. That one phone call, seriously, that is all it took to turn us back around. It still amazes me. As I am sitting here sharing this with you, I realize that it was only 11 months ago. That one phone call fixed so many things. Melvin has this magical, uncanny gift to talk to people at a level that I know God must be talking through him.

He was able to reach Tim where he was at. Once we talked through the situation, Melvin started asking the pointed questions. I came to find out that Tim had lost his way to a point. Tim did not really know how to show his love for me in the way that connected with my heart. He showed love, yes, and it was in the way he knew best. However, it was not in the way that spoke to my heart. Tim had to learn a few new things to talk heart to heart with me. Melvin asked, "So, Tim, would it help you if you had a list of 10 things from Tammy, a list that she writes up that tells you how she wants to feel loved by you?"

Tim started nodding his head yes. I could really feel and I saw how the invisible pressure was lifting from him. I could see him relax a bit more knowing now he would have a go-to list. When his mind was blank, he would have a list that he could rely on to help him on his path to loving me more. That is really what he wanted, but at times, he just didn't know how. Tim needed help, and neither one of us even knew it. We didn't know how, or why.

Then Melvin starts to share with me about me. Yep, really, he did have to tell me, "Tammy, with all the intense work you have done on yourself, even before I have known you for well over a decade, darling, it is you. You will be the one that for right now will be the leader of your relationship. Tim requires time to catch up to you. For right now, Tammy, most of the time, you will be carrying the weight. Tammy, I know you can do this. Tammy, I believe in you. You got this girl!"

One of the most important things I have learned in the last couple of years in regards to how we communicate with others is that sometimes people do not hear us, actually, most of the time they do not. They are too busy formulating their reply to really listen. Do you ever catch yourself doing that? Seriously, pay attention to how you are communicating and be in the present moment and watch yourself if you are already thinking about a reply before the other person is done talking. If so, then you are not truly hearing what the other person is saying. We all need to learn active listening, allowing our mind not to worry about a comeback until the other person is done sharing.

Sometimes we don't say things out loud, going over and over a scenario, playing it back in our minds, how each step piece by piece is going. Our imagining of it all can be so real that we think we have said what we are thinking. For the message to be received it has to be spoken at a listening time. Sometimes, things are said at a non-listening moment.

Communication can be hard and scary, especially when sharing at deep levels, sharing our real truth, never really knowing how the other person is going to react. We cannot let that stop us though. Remember, what you do not say with words will show up with actions. Do you realize that your eyes communicate way more than any words can? Your energy and your attitude can also communicate what the unspoken word really wants to come out and say. I invite you to have the bravery it takes to step into your communication with a new commitment of being real and saying truth with your words.

Life does not always happen in neat little boxes. How can I expect my husband to hear me when I am not clear in what I am saying? Life can be messy, and it does not allow us to stand back and only work on our relationship. Tim's head can be pretty full with working a fulltime job being the supervisor of a road construction crew and taking care of the farm on the weekends. When the cattle need attention, when a calf needs to be warmed-up or a sick cow needs to be loaded and taken to the vet, it does not mean he is not committed to our relationship. Sometimes life can get in the way. I think that learning to communicate better, both of us, was our biggest obstacle and our highest priority, even though neither of us saw it at the time, not to the degree that we have now learned.

Having the thought, "if he loves me enough he will know, he will just know what to do and how to do it," a thought I had for sooooo much of our married life, I was setting myself up for disappointment. That rarely exists with me anymore, and if it does start to come up, I catch it quicker now. I still continue, as does Tim, to deprogram the old way of things and reprogram ourselves with better skills in all areas of life.

Some people may already know these things, but in my experience and as a result of thousands of conversations, those people are few and far between. Most of us have to develop that trait in ourselves and in others. First, we need to be open to it and start to work on it. I no longer have that "if he loved me enough he would know" attitude. That in itself I call *freedom!*

Where my responsibility and accountability comes in is that I have to tell Tim exactly how I am feeling. For example, I need to say, "Tim, if the lights do not go up, that will really hurt my feelings. Tim, I need to know that you take our relationship seriously and do not allow yourself to backslide. I need to know that I am still number one with you. By putting up the lights, you make me feel so loved and really important to you on levels that are new to me and it feels really really good." If I had said that, or something close to it, I am sure he would have gotten how important it was.

Remember, people cannot read our minds. We need to quit expecting people to read between the lines. Our husbands want to know how to take care of us, what our needs and wants and desires are. They want that list, even if they don't use it. I think it is more about having a back-up plan. It's like having money in the bank, *ahhh, no more stress, I have a love account.* More ideas and actions start to show up and come out, and you ladies will be the beneficiaries of the deliciousness that is waiting for you. Speak up and share. It is worth it. Do not let fear or anger keep you from sharing your truth.

CHAPTER 23

Real Communication

Ahhhhh, taking a deep breath, a year later, and it is our first time ever to be alone on Christmas morning.

Learning what I did from the year before, knowing now that I have to be very clear with my communication, there were no subtle hints. My husband was very much aware after I thoroughly explained the importance of the lights down the 300 foot driveway being up and working. At first, when I share my thoughts and feelings, I am not sure he hears me. That is sometimes how our communication goes. I think he did, he says he did, yet at times I do wonder, even still today, as we are really still getting to know each other on new levels of understanding and sharing.

At times, and it is becoming more frequent, it seems we can read each other's minds. For example, for days after I shared the importance of the driveway lights, I kept noticing the lights were not up. Before I could say something to Tim about it, he came to me. I want to repeat this, because this still is a whole new way of being together — Tim came to me to share his concerns. He explained, "Tammy, I was thinking about how much you want the lights up. However, we have more hay to haul home yet. Because of the wide loads, I really do not want to take any chances of the trailer hitting the lights and knocking them down once they are up. We sure do not need lights to be torn or run over. We will put them up once we are done hauling bales home, ok?"

Wow, I was overjoyed with Tim for coming to me to explain. He initiated the conversation; this was something new to me, to us. When he explained to me I completely understood. And, shssssh, don't tell Tim, but I was so deeply touched by his efforts for me to know his concern about making me happy with the lights going up and staying up and not to being damaged, that honestly, it no longer really mattered if the driveway lights went up. He shared his thoughts and feelings with me on his own. I did not have to prompt him to do so. Do you realize how much that really meant to my heart and my soul? Another level of connection was happening. I was feeling valued and respected by my husband.

Our eldest daughter, Crystal, moved out of our home in February 2016 with our grandson Chase, who we had helped raise so she could finish college and start her career. As Crystal was a single mom and a senior in college when she had Chase, we wanted to make sure she stayed in school and graduated.

Now, for the first time in 36 years, we were going to be waking up alone on Christmas morning. It seems a bit weird, but I have tears in my eyes as I think about it — ok, it would be only the two of us now. What would we consciously do to celebrate our Christmas morning and start a new tradition with the two of us?

People talk about being an empty nester, and now that is what we were: Tim and I, the two of us, embracing each other more than ever on our second start this Christmas morning of 2016. Thinking about it was bittersweet, knowing Chase would not be with us, sharing the excitement of a child on Christmas morning. Hmmm, I guess I might just have to make up for that excitement. The younger girl n me was also giggling with excitement … giggle.

For the last 30 plus years, while working fulltime, Tim's only time off was in December. During those three weeks he would attempt to catch up on the things he needed to do, a never-ending task of course. Also Tim was usually frustrated by the cold weather preventing him doing a lot of things he wanted to get done.

I had been feeling that there was something very special about this Christmas. People kept saying to me, "This year is special for you and Tim. Tammy, make this Christmas really be about you and Tim." I was noticing that for most people who have their own business, this time of the year is about sales and ending the year with a big bang.

Well, my business was different. I was delivering a keynote for the local university graduating class, I was preparing for a workshop I was presenting in February, along with coaching my clients and welcoming new ones on board. Yet above all things, I was creating and working to have a very special Christmas season, decorating more than ever, spending time with family in ways that touched all the ages, especially my 11 grandchildren, from 7 months to 14 years old, playing board games and card games. All of us were coming together to decorate, with Tim helping this year more than he ever had in the past.

Maybe I was not doing 'business' like most others, and that was ok. I really felt that what was more important was to follow the guidance of my heart, my spirit, my soul. I let those three things determine my direction, and when I do so, I know all will be in Divine order.

I talked with Tim about how important that Christmas season was, because it was about the two of us being the most important thing to each other. It was about creating new, precious memories, new experiences that were full of joy, fun and laughter. I heard many years ago that it takes five great things to happen to dull out one painful thing. The more we made great things happen in all ways that Christmas, the more they diminished the hurtful moments of the previous year.

Tim heard me. He had listened and he heard me. He split up his chores. He was communicating with me when something came up. Here was a man who had done the same thing for over 30 years, been in charge and responsible for dozens of people in heavy highway danger zone asphalt road construction. He was going to do it again, the same routine in December, because it was such a habit. He never even thought of the fact that he no longer worked at his job. Now, he had the opportunity to change the way of doing things around the farm, which opened up more time for the two of us. We were doing things together preparing for the holiday season. This taught me again that there are times in our lives when we are so used to doing the same thing over and over and over again, that it takes someone to bring it to our attention so we can change it up and do something different.

In my golden years, when I am sitting in my rocking chair out on the porch and I am telling my great great grandchildren stories of my life, they will be the new stories, the stories that Tim and I are creating now. They will be of love and commitment, and perseverance and permission to be angry, even at God. The stories will be about how miracles really do happen. And I will tell them, "Believe in miracles, expect miracles and you will see miracles, and even be part of those miracles." The fact that Tim and I were thriving in our second start, in our new relationship, married for over 37 years, after a near divorce only three short years before, was a true miracle.

You cannot assume the other person knows how much you care about them. You have got to open up to their way of wanting to be loved. You have got to get out of your mind and into your heart and figure it out. Quit being lazy about love and start listening to your partner. Figure it out, read books, do some research, hire a coach, learn their love language and speak it to them. That is one of the best ways to fill up their love bucket and yours too. That is another area that I help my clients with.

Tim and I are really listening to each other. We are hearing each other. Sometimes I really have to be careful not to let my mind wonder and think the thoughts like, "Damn, why didn't this happen sooner, so much pain would have been avoided." Those thoughts make me cry at times. I pull myself back to the present and realize we did the best we could with what we had at the time.

Now, yes now, we are finding each other all over again, most of the time. Before I go out the door, Tim starts my car to let it warm up. Tim helps me with my coat. Tim carries my bags for me to the car. Tim is more attentive to me than ever before, and it is because he desires to be that way, and it is up to me to share with him if I ever feel as if I am not being taken care of the way I desire him to do.

When I was outside working on putting up the Christmas lights, Tim checked on me, asking me how it was going, getting his coat on and coming outside to help, asking me, "What can I do for you?" Ohhh, this new Tim, well he was helping me to fall in love with him on a whole new level. Ahhhh, Christmas love. It was just me and Tim now. Before this year, Crystal always took it upon herself to be in charge of the outside Christmas lights. She was my special Christmas Elf. Now, it was up to Tim and me, we were coming together on another area of life. Tim was helping me with something that means an incredible amount to me.

When Tim showed me that he was thinking about the lights, that spoke volumes to me. That in itself was saying to me "I love you Tammy, I really love you." It moved me very deeply. I knew that he heard me, he was processing, and he was coming up with a new idea, a new way of doing things that would make it good all ways around.

When there is the right kind of communication, when we are clear, even when we are scared, when the other person can hear you, the two of you can realize something pretty incredible. When life is messy, we need to cut the other person some slack. Most importantly, we have to continually communicate clearly; this needs to be an ongoing practice. Remember to also give yourself some slack. Do not so be so hard on yourself. Be kind to you.

Having the Christmas miracle all year long, living that miracle every day, is what I truly believe our marriage is now.

CHAPTER 24

The Greatest Present

I always dreamt of a relationship like this, and I'm now realizing it in my marriage in a continual flow. Things are going so wonderfully. Yes, we do still have those moments when we get on each other's nerves, those moments of misunderstanding. Most of the time, they come and go without the triggers and depth of pain that were once felt. We are quicker to bring them to light, discuss them, apologize if we feel the need to, and move on. Wow, no more grudge-holding. We are really, really healing the past relationship, and we are not even intending to. The more we are creating this incredible second start on our new relationship, the more the old hurts are healing. They are dissipating with time as if they never existed. And, I am learning more about myself and the times when I do get on edge. The reason for it is usually when I feel Tim is not initiating enough or not stepping outside of his comfort box enough.

There are so many silver linings to working on our new relationship. It is also healing both of us in ways that are unexpected. I know this to be true for myself.

I share with Tim my deep desire to finish writing my book — only two chapters to go and wanting to be completed with the writing by December 16 — and even though it isn't his project, he is very supportive and encouraging. If I get distracted or pulled away for any reasons around the house, he urges me to "get back to writing" in a loving manner. I crack up laughing, as at times he has a sort of stern tone to his voice. Ah, deep breath, Tim is really is supporting me, really truly supporting me, and I feel it. I feel it in the depths of my heart and soul. Yes, he is filling my love bucket.

If something happens to pull us apart for a bit, we both sense it, and so much quicker. The other day, on Sunday, we were expecting friends out for a special supper that Tim always makes when they come to visit once a year. Tim got delayed longer than expected as he was helping two of our daughters, Tara and Crystal; they were all out hunting for their deer. So, I started supper. Was it in my plans to do so? No it wasn't. So, it's a change of plans. Jenna was helping me out in the kitchen and we began to prepare the meal. I started cooking, and when Tim came home he wanted to take over. "Ohhhh no, don't touch my pan, I am the cook in the moment." I was concentrating. People were hungry, and the potatoes were taking longer than expected. I was a bit frazzled wanting to get the food done quickly, wanting to make sure everyone was taken care of. I was frying up the pheasant that Jenna spent over an hour cleaning. "Don't mess with my meat, ha ha ha." Ok, I was laughing then, but apparently I was so focused on feeding everyone, that I guess I was a bit snippy when I told Tim to back away from the frying pan.

I didn't mean to be that way and did not catch myself in the moment. When I was finished and my pan was empty, a hot flash hit me, and I did ask him to take over. I had to go stand by the door to get myself cooled off.

The next morning Tim approached me, saying to me with a very concerned tone to his voice, "Thanks so much for taking over cooking last night. I am sorry I made you mad. I was out with the girls later than I expected to be." "Oh, I wasn't mad, I was in the zone. You know how that is Tim, when we are cooking and we don't want the other one to mess with our creation," and I winked at him. "I am sorry if you thought I was mad at you. I certainly was not." I went over and hugged him from behind and whispered in his ear, "I was really ok about cooking last night, and I was glad you were out helping our daughters." And then I reached around and kissed him on the cheek.

We talk about things so much quicker, within minutes or hours. No longer does it go more than a full day. And now, and get this, because this is huge in our relationship, *now*, Tim initiates much more than he ever did. Well actually he never really did at all, and now he does. He starts the conversations, even the tough ones. I am celebrating this action, because this one action alone tells me he is invested in us, tells me that he cares about us, shows me that it is not only on my shoulders anymore. Tim makes me feel like the queen in our kingdom even more when he initiates things. This is unity; this is the two of us making it happen.

Let's face it, I am here to tell you, I do want to be taken care of, and that is ok. Can I take care of myself? Sure, you bet I can. There are times though when I want to know my man can take care of me, especially in the busiest, most productive times that come along. I need to know that he is there for me as much if not more than I am there for him — to pick up some slack, to help me free up time in my schedule. Possibly this comes from never feeling I was taken care of as a child, or even the fact that I put so much into our family, our kids and grandchildren. Who knows where it comes from. I know this is part of what I desire, and ladies, that does not make me weak. It actually makes me stronger to know this about myself and realize it and help Tim to understand this part of me. And I continue to learn and understand about myself.

I say we are doing exceptionally well, and it feels so incredible. This alone is one of the greatest Christmas presents Tim could ever give me. This, how we are right now, you cannot buy this. You cannot go into a store and pick off the shelf the different ingredients to put into a relationship and expect to mix it all together and let it bake on its own. A can of this and a package of that, a carton this and a pinch of that.

Here he is surprising me again, initiating a date night. Tim asked me to clear my calendar for Thursday night, to please be on time, so he can take me out. I don't know where yet, but that doesn't matter as much as the fact that it was his idea, and he surprised me. I told him how much it means to me when he initiates and he heard me. He not only listened, he heard. That is what is really important. He is the one planning something. Here is another example. He is the one who cleaned up the boxes that held all of the outside Christmas decorations, enough so I can drive into the garage. He told me, "Tammy, I do not expect you to park outside, to have to go outside to start your car and let it warm up every single morning." We were going to clean up all the totes and boxes together, and it never happened, and he surprised me by doing it himself for me. We are doing this magical dance. The dance of starting over and creating this new relationship that we both desire. He is taking care of me better as his queen and the woman of the family.

This is so incredibly huge. This is showing how important it is to communicate and share how important it is for me to share my feelings. We are doing the dance in life, in our relationship, and before long, fingers crossed, we will take it to the dance floor. Ok that makes me giggle. Maybe I can get Tim to take a dance class with me. Now that would be a miracle! Dancing is my passion but not so much his.

Believe in your dreams; they can and do come true. This is for real. It is not a dream anymore. This is the closest we have been in our 37 years of marriage. This is the possibility of what can truly happen in a relationship when both parties are working on and in the relationship. Especially with honest clear communication, the possibilities are endless. When Tim and I would go to weddings and I would see older couples gliding across the dance floor with ease and grace, enjoying each other, I would have tears in my eyes. I wanted to be that couple, holding hands, laughing together, being with each other with so much joy. Getting old together and enjoying it. That dream is coming true. Maybe you could say our second start on our relationship is our dance floor in life. We are swaying and gliding and moving in ways we never have before, and we share who has the lead, and it feels really good that Tim has taken that lead so much lately.

This is a legacy that we are living, not just leaving. Our children, grandchildren and generations to come will know and feel the legacy of the energy of what we are creating. They will know what it takes to make relationships work in all areas of life. This is real, there is no pretense anymore at this second start. When you get over the hump of pretense and find the courage to be real with each other, what you can create is incredible. When both people work on it, both people commit, it is incredible what can be realized. People really want this. You don't know how you affect other people when you quit pretending and start being about what is going on in life. The pain is real, the confusion is real, stuff does happen. So what are we going to do about it? Let's get real people; together we can do this. I am here for you. Don't think you can make this happen on your own, not if you truly want to make shift happen. You do that with someone guiding you along the way.

I love living in my home now. I absolutely love it so much that at times, I literally have to force myself to leave. Especially right now, I want to be in my home with all the ambiance of the Christmas season and all the decorations, with all the beauty surrounding me. Once Tim and I started working on our home together, and I started to feel this is my home now, I no longer dreaded going home. Sometimes I just laugh. I get giddy about how miraculous things continue to shift and change around.

Create your home as if you are going on a vacation. Set it up like the vacation you want to be on. Create that essence in your own home and your surrounding area, so every time you are at home you feel to some extent like you are on holiday. I don't need to go and see amazing Christmas decorations. I enjoy what we all created right here in our own home.

Listen closely please. I really desire you to hear this. I had to share with Tim how much it means to me when he initiates. I had to stand up, open up and allow myself to be vulnerable and for goodness sake no longer think he can read my mind. I had to share with him how I feel when he is the one who initiates things, no matter what they are. Even Tim emptying the dishwasher without me asking is an aphrodisiac to some degree. It is whenever Tim does something for me, for us, something that takes a bit of a load off of my shoulders. The tingle in my heart grows and shines bright. When he surprises me with an unexpected date, when he is so matter of fact about me putting time in my schedule, I feel this, "I got this covered Tammy," energy. I can relax, do my work, keep creating and work on the projects I am bringing forth, knowing Tim is taking care of whatever needs to be taken care of. The communication and respect that continues to grow for each other is unparalleled.

CHAPTER 25

Creating Heaven on Earth

With all I shared in this book, I do still understand that sometimes a marriage cannot be saved. I have seen enough of this to realize that, and I do not make light of it. I really did not think my marriage could be saved. I had no clue. Sometimes we are with the wrong person. It may not be the right two people. Sometimes there has been too much pain that went too deep and one cannot recover from it. Sometimes there was too much collateral damage to resurrect the broken pieces and put them back together again. Possibly both people in the relationship are not equally dedicated to really making things work. This happens, especially if there has been some major pain involved. Being in pain that is not taken care of can take you out of the dance of relationships. This is the truth for some.

Then there are those times when a marriage can be saved, even when we think it is hopeless and we feel as if we are done and too tired, plain ole too worn out to go on. Sometimes there is too much at stake to walk away. If you really try, it takes tearing down the walls and opening yourself up. Believe me, I know it is not easy. This can be so much to ask for, yet it does take showing vulnerability to heal, and it can be scary to do this. I am not here to sugar-coat this. I share this all with the utmost love and respect for where you are in life and to let you know that this can be tough stuff at times and I understand that. And opening up is what it takes to really heal, to heal and be free. In the end it is worth it. Oh my, the rewards and the blessings are beyond anything you can possibly imagine. It does take having faith as small as a mustard seed.

It also takes that outside influence of wisdom and at times tough love. It takes a village, a tribe, a community to come together to help us through the most difficult times, to help us save our relationship. We had friends encouraging us. We had cheerleaders rooting for us. We had family helping us along the way. We had counselors Melvin and Sherrie to guide us. They were like the Elders in the tribe, helping us break down the walls of resistance to facing the unknown and showing us a new way of being with each other. There is no way we could have done this alone. It not only takes a village to raise a child, it takes one to help all members of that village. We needed our own tribe around us, protecting us, as we started to heal, open and build on our second start.

The truth will set you free. No other statement I know has more validity than this one. People really want the truth, even when it is not what they want to hear. Without the truth there is nothing. Living under false pretenses is living in Hell on Earth.

Living in your truth is living in Heaven on Earth.

Imagine, there is no more hiding. You can be all of who you really are. For Tim and me, we came out of hiding the day I walked out. The truth came to the surface. The pretense that everything was ok melted away, and we did not even realize that there was any pretense. It was just the way we ended up being. That was part of what was exhausting me. Ah, the pretense was gone. Then, life began again. The real meaning of living in Heaven on

Earth was starting to be within our reach. We were starting to learn that.

It can be scary letting others see your vulnerability, seeing the truth of your relationship when it is in shambles — knowing you can be judged, not knowing how others will respond to you, even if they will still talk to you. Opening yourself up not just to each other, but to yourself. For some people, it is seeing yourself for the first time ever in your life, uncovering what has been hidden in the deep crevices of life. I completely understand how scary this can be.

You have got to have support. Do not do this alone. This is one of the reasons I am so committed to being the best possible coach and mentor. You have got to reach out, and sometimes it takes reaching out over and over again. And sometimes, it takes getting pissed off about what is happening, and screaming out for help. Most importantly in my experience, it takes listening to the answers that come to you, and especially being open to when those answers come, because at times they appear in ways that are not the way we think they are supposed to be. Be open to new ways of thinking and being and doing. I encourage you, be open.

Ah, to breathe again, knowing there is no more hiding. I realized that I was not breathing to the depth of what I could. Starting to walk in my truth was like the relief of coming up for air. There are people who look at Tim and me, and realize for themselves, *if they can do it, I can too.* Now I can be me, no longer hiding, no longer pretending at any level, the free and open and loving me, living in integrity step by step, to continue the healing on so many levels, and helping others to do the same. And knowing this is the beginning of great things to come. Starting to really understand the meaning of living in Heaven on Earth, because that is what I am creating. I know and feel this to be true. This is what I help others to create.

The true test of the pudding was our coming back together, our working on and creating new levels of communication in our marriage, our saying yes to each other and building a new relationship. Most importantly, this is something we are showing in real time to not only our five children and their significant others, also as important if not more so, to our 11 grandchildren. I feel more than anything that we are now truly a living legacy of healing, not just leaving a legacy but living it in the current moment. This is what really matters. They will have this strength, this determination, this willpower, this commitment, this faith, all that and more that is beyond explanation, running through their blood not only within them also for all future generations. They come from True Grit and True Love. They come from Truth. There is no greater gift to pass on to our current and future generations. The tough work is worth it. It does pay off. The truth will set you free. And the legacy of healing continues.

Women, Your Time Is Now – Your Sisters Are waiting for You to arrive!

Be *all* the woman you are called to be. The world is waiting for you. Your soul is waiting for you. Together as we explore your hopes, dreams, desires and where you are stuck in life, I use my expert skills and intuitive abilities allowing Divine wisdom and guidance to come through and assist you in unveiling you to you in the areas of your life you choose to work on.

Come as you are, because who you are right now is enough in this moment. This is where you start as you work with me one-on-one, as we connect on many levels. We explore areas of your life to shine the light on what is hiding from you in the shadows. We connect with your soul, your passion and your purpose to inspire and empower you.

Finally there is a safe haven for *you* to become all you came here to be, do, have and create.

There are no limitations of where we can work together, from your personal life to your business, from spiritual to physical, from sexuality to relationships. It is time to *know your power* and embrace it, to make *shift* happen and breakthrough what has been holding you back in any area of life.

I am a beacon of *light* and will shine this on the shadows of the unknown as together we explore and reveal your hidden gifts, talents and more, in order for you to bring up and out your full self-expression.

You start to *value who you are* on all levels of your life. You are woman, you deserve to be honored and respected. It is time to step into your power, to live a life in *full-out joy*. It's your time to shine!

You are tired. Come, it is time for you to be heard, be seen, be nurtured, be held. Recharge and be shown the possibilities that you choose for *your* highest and greatest self to *shine ever so brightly.*

I am here and by your side every step of the way.

I have limited availability for the outrageously over the top one-on one mentoring program Creating your Heaven on Earth. Inspiring women to get out of overwhelm, be empowered, gain clarity, live joyously and more.

Go here to apply to work with me: www.transformintojoy.com/book/

You are required to fill out an application before booking a time so I know if you are committed to doing the work. It is not always easy. However, together, we can make it fun! I look forward to connecting with you when we get on a call to see if working together is the right and perfect thing for you and your soul.

Women — Your Time is NOW — JOYOUS HUGS

Tammy Lee Schumacher www.transformintojoy.com

Women's Empowerment Mentor ~ Intuitive JOY Expert ~ Reinvention Life Strategist

Testimonials

"MAKE SHIFT HAPPEN" with Tammy Lee Opened Me Up To More and ME and MY Life!!

"Tammy Lee has been a true inspiration for me! I have always viewed a coach as someone who teaches me to perform better in a sport or challenging subject. Her expert coaching has assisted and gently guided me to improve MYSELF. The most important thing any one person could do. Her professionalism, insight, and intuition has encouraged me to TRUST what I was feeling, SEEK what I was lacking, and EXPLORE what was my greatest potential. Her joyful spirit of helping me find my inner CELEBRATION was not always easy, but through time…I found it. The joy of celebrating me, my life, and my inner goddess. Through her mentoring and coaching, my life has opened up many possibilities and doors personally, and professionally. Thank YOU, Tammy Lee ☺"

Ceena Owens BGS, RN, BCTMB l
Director of Massage Therapy l Fort Hays State University

Taking the Energy of Our Business to HIGHER Levels, with FUN!

"Tammy reached out to me with a warm open heart and helped me with such grace! I am so grateful to have her in my life. I am now feeling so good about my business copy that she looked over with me and reminded me to look at it from a energetic view point. I see myself as seeing in energy but I felt as though Tammy took it to a new level for me! Thank

you Tammy for all the laughs, everything you touch becomes fun again as you put your whole heart and soul into everything you do. Yes, even business copy becomes fun with Tammy!!!

LOVE PRISCILLA & PATRICK ....ps....I can't speak of
Tammy Lee Schumacher highly enough, she's 'the real deal' X

"MY BUSINESS TRIPLED In LESS THAN 60 Days!!!

It meant the world to me as a single mother, raising my son on my own and a business owner, working with Tammy Lee is one of the best investments I have ever made!!!

SARA BOYD, owner, Tresses Salon

You bring us to a SAFE HAVEN!

Tammy, it are Safe to talk to you about anything. Never feel I am being judged. You make people feel good about themselves (their situation)- and therefore bring out the best in people. Self Confidence/ esteem. Unconditional support / non judgmental

Gift of laughter- add humor and therefore stress relief! Patient Brighten/ Lighten up one environment/state of mind etc.

I love you Tammy, Go get 'em!!!!! (I desire to remain anonymous)

My Voice Is Stronger and My Energy Flowing

I'm pleased to be writing a testimonial of Tammy's skills as an intuitive who clears chakra energy. We had just met and were engaged in a casual conversation, which, as the topics shifted, turned into a rather intense exploration of my beliefs and feelings.

At one point Tammy asked me, "do you find yourself making excuses for other people a lot?" I had to think a minute and then answered, "Yes." She then explained about her challenges with the throat chakra and how blocking emotions and thoughts interferes with the vocal chords. Instead of a strong, clear voice, you can end up with a scratchy, squeaky, or non-existent voice. You might have to constantly clear your throat, and not because of allergies.

Tammy's questions were challenging, but not invasive. I felt uncomfortable because this was territory that I had been in denial about, but when she used the word "excuse," I knew that this conversation was about truth and not denying reality. The next day when I saw Tammy I thanked her for the conversation and for clearing my throat chakra.

I'm aware of chakras, but I don't really work with them. After my conversation with Tammy, I felt more energy flowing, and my voice was stronger. I felt that a burden of Silence and denial had been lifted from my heart, which made the energy flow to my throat. We met and had this healing encounter in April. It's now July, and I remember our conversation and continue to benefit from what she told me. She connected with me and seemed to see my emotional body or chakras and guided me to a state of greater clarity and health.

Thank you, Tammy for your insights and laughter, and the change for the better!

I Highly recommend you!

DIANE BARKER

"She Is Your SAFE HAVEN"

Tammy has been a friend of mine for all of my adult life. She has Always inspired me!!!

I have met up with Tammy again and just visiting with her. I have gotten a new approach to taking care of "ME"! She is so easy to talk to and always makes you feel like she is your "SAFE HAVEN" She is a God-Send!!

SANDY

TAMMY LEE SCHUMACHER

"The Go To Woman to 'Make SHIFT Happen' "

"I am committed to Impact and Empower 5 Billion people, with an experience of Core Confidence and Connection to their Unique Joy through Trust, Truth and Divine Self-Expression."
TAMMY LEE SCHUMACHER

www.transformintoJOY.com

More Praise for
"The Second Start"

"The Second Start is like having a long, luscious chat with a trusted friend. The personal stories Tammy shares leave you feeling not so alone and not afraid to step fully into living your life. It's full of caring, good words of wisdom that can only come from someone who has "been there". It's well written and engaging...I couldn't put it down!"

– JANCY

Tammy,

I downloaded your book on Tuesday and finished it last night! Wow!!! I have to say that I was hesitant to even start because I didn't know if I could read about your second start with your husband. 3 years ago this time I was seriously contemplating leaving my marriage. We had obstacles that I could not see over or around. I stuck to it, mostly out of fear. 2 ½ years ago I woke up to find my husband deceased. I didn't want to read your book because I thought it would bring back all the regret I've been dealing with for not getting my second start at a better marriage. I took the chance and I'm so glad I did. In the last 2 ½ years I have lost not only my husband, my marriage, my security but now I am in the middle of a foreclosure that will leave me with little of the life we built over 20 years together. Talk about fear! What I took from your book was that I get a chance to make a second start and I am determined to shed the fear and move forward to see what this life has in store for me. Thank you so much for the encouragement!

Much love,
HEATHER BITTER

"I couldn't stop reading. There are so many parts of this book that completely relate to my own life. What a great outlook and thought process of turning things around. I always say there is a reason I am guided to see or read something and this is just what I needed to read at this moment in my life."

– N.B.

"I knew Tammy growing up. She was the mom that us girls wanted on our girl scout trips and school trips. This book really opened up my eyes. I cried and laughed. This book reached out to me. Most of it was like a reflection of my feelings my whole life. People read this book. Tammy will open your eyes. Thank you Tammy for being a beacon for women."

– Jessica

"The Second Start is such an Inspirational and an Awesome Journey!!! I downloaded this book on Sunday and couldn't put it down until I had the whole book read! I highly recommend this book to everyone! Tammy Lee has poured out her heart and soul in this book and shows what determination can do for a marriage and family and how she is willing to fight for others who are struggling in communicating and to bringing JOY into their life! Thank you Tammy Lee for sharing your story with the world!!!"

– Dar Rae

"Tammy's book is definitely written straight from the heart. She wrote about what many people struggle with in life and relationships but don't ever have the courage or strength to address or fix. I know as a busy wife and mom of 5 who has definitely had some struggles in life, I can definitely relate to alot of what Tammy shares. I was very inspired by her words, her positive outlook and her perseverance."

– LDM

"What a story. We know this story is all around us. We rarely can read and see the story unfold in front of us. What a privilege to read the Story of Tammy Lee Schumacher. It has been even more of a privilege to know her. Thanks for what you did for all of us Tam but most of Thanks for being willing to serve the cause of God by helping feed His sheep. "If you love me, feed my sheep."

– DMW

"Such an inspiring book, so many parts I found myself relating to as if it was me. This book was one of those that once you start reading you can't stop reading, an inspiration that no matter what life hands you, you yourself have the power to overcome, change and find happiness."

– MARLA ORTH

"This book isn't something you'll be able to put down and finish days later. You'll binge read it. Amazing story, very inspirational!"

"Love this book! So glad Tammy chose to share her story with the world instead of just those of us she has touched in her life."

– CHARLENE L.

67142186R00116

Made in the USA
Lexington, KY
03 September 2017